Wiley's

CHAMPIONSHIP

BBQ

Wiley's
CHAMPIONSHIP
BBQ

SECRETS THAT OLD MEN
TAKE TO THE GRAVE

WILEY McCRARY 🔥 JANET McCRARY 🔥 AMY PAIGE CONDON

Photographs by CHIA CHONG

GIBBS SMITH
TO ENRICH AND INSPIRE HUMANKIND

First Edition
18 17 16 15 14   5 4 3 2 1

Published by
Gibbs Smith
P.O. Box 667
Layton, Utah 84041

1.800.835.4993 orders
www.gibbs-smith.com

Designed by Andrew Brozyna
Printed and bound in China
Gibbs Smith books are printed on either recycled, 100% post-consumer
waste, FSC-certified papers or on paper produced from sustainable PEFC-
certified forest/controlled wood source. Learn more at www.pefc.org.

Library of Congress Cataloging-in-Publication Data

ISBN 13: 978-1-4236-3631-1

From Wiley and Janet to Miss Alberta, Big Jim, and Ed and Muriel Roith: Thank you for teaching us everything we needed to know about cooking and barbecue. You changed our lives.

From Wiley to Janet: Without your encouragement, I may never have entered that first contest and realized my dream of owning a restaurant.

From Janet to Wiley: Thank you for showing me that food is all about passion and adventure.

From Amy to Brian: Thank you for choosing passion over convenience, faith over security, hope over certainty. With deepest love and gratitude, Ms. Cakes.

"Have you found joy in your life?
Has your life brought joy to others?"
—Carter Chambers in *The Bucket List*

CONTENTS

PREFACE 9

INTRODUCTION 11

SEASONINGS AND SPICES 27

COW AND LAMB 51

PIG 85

BIRD 101

FISH AND CRUSTACEANS 117

VEGETABLES AND STARCHES 143

SUGAR, BUTTER, AND FLOUR 183

LIBATIONS 201

HELPFUL RESOURCES 206

ACKNOWLEDGMENTS 209

ABOUT THE AUTHORS 211

INDEX OF RECIPES 213

PREFACE

"You like barbecue?" he asked as I took a seat next to his at the bar—the only chair open at the pocket-sized joint located in a nondescript strip mall on Whitemarsh Island in Savannah, Georgia. The man was seated in a director's chair with "The BBQ General" stencilled across the back, and I wondered if he was also the owner of the red pickup truck parked out front with a vanity plate that read, "DRBBQ." He wore a red trucker hat, and a soggy, unlit cigar hung from the corner of his mouth. The wide lenses of his glasses magnified blue eyes that glinted with mischief.

Those three words opened up an easy conversation between Wiley McCrary and me that continued for a year's worth of afternoons, Saturday morning breakfasts, and BBQ 101 classes. As we discussed the flavors that different woods impart and compared the virtues of gas versus charcoal, Wiley and I—despite a generational divide—became friends. So many times he made me repeat his mantra, "Internal temperature always prevails over time," the phrase now permeates my neural pathways. Over those long, meandering conversations, we shared recipes, swapped stories, and talked about the meaning of "place." Although I had grown up in the mecca of barbecue—the great state of Texas, where beef and mesquite reign—I discovered, through innumerable samplings at Wiley's counter, that I was drawn to pork and sweet, tomatoey sauces. If barbecue were a birthright, I might actually hail from St. Louis . . . or maybe Kansas City.

Wiley is more democratic. He does not favor one region over another. He loves them all. With more than thirty years spent honing the craft of 'cue, Wiley has become an evangelist, devoting his adult life to teaching and preaching the good news gospel of the Church of the Holy Smoke. He has converted many, if the awards on his wall are any testament: two dinner bells as grand champion at national barbecue competitions, a Louisville Slugger for first place in ribs, and plaques from the *National Barbecue News* hailing his small shop as one of the top barbecue

9

restaurants in the nation. Wiley himself is not prone to braggadòcio, though, so his patrons speak on his behalf, rating his food consistently within the top five on TripAdvisor in Savannah on more than one occasion, and returning him time and again to the top of every "Best of Savannah" readers' poll.

Wiley has always wanted to write a cookbook, but not a "good ol' boy one," he instructed. He wanted to dispel myths and mysteries, he said, and to teach people what they were capable of doing on their own. This cookbook is a result of all those conversations we shared, and it provides more than a collection of recipes. As it recounts the story of a life in barbecue, it offers the wisdom Wiley gained in the trenches of running a catering business, an eatery, and a national award-winning competition barbecue team. While we readers may not end up with a rail cart full of trophies like Wiley, we may still become the champions of our own backyards if we just surrender to the pit master.

—Amy Paige Condon
Savannah, Georgia

INTRODUCTION

When you're on the road with a pit and an RV, you develop knowledge of where you'd be welcome to park. Several years ago, I was driving back to Atlanta from a barbecue competition in Alabama when I saw a Cracker Barrel sitting off the highway. I was hungry and tired and needed a break. A pit acts like a billboard, and no sooner had I parked and stepped down from the cab than a gentleman approached, waving his arms wildly and smiling like he had just won the lottery.

"I see you're in barbecue," he said as he drew closer.

I nodded.

"I make the best homemade barbecue sauce you ever tasted."

I've always enjoyed learning new things. I'm somewhat of a foodie and like to taste dishes from all over the world, especially from home cooks and backyarders who carry with them knowledge of ingredients and techniques passed from one generation to the next. Some of the best cooks in America never went to culinary school; they simply learned standing next to a grandmother in her kitchen or beside an uncle who built his own barbecue pit out of a recycled drum.

I asked the man if he had any sauce I could try. He didn't.

I asked him if he'd mind sharing the recipe with me so that I could make it somewhere down the road and let him know how I liked it.

His enthusiasm flagged. "I can't tell you that," he said, almost offended. "It's a secret."

I've lived in barbecue a long time. That man probably will take to his grave a really good recipe, and nobody will ever get to enjoy it after he's gone. That's a shame. I wish I could tell you he was the first person who had refused to share his ideas with me, but . . . I have gotten used to his kind of tease.

Barbecue is surrounded by myths, folklore, and downright lies. The truth is that although barbecue is an art form based on good craftsmanship, the skills are transferable. The wheel can be reinvented only so many times. We, who've gone before, owe it to the universe to teach you, just the way someone taught us. I couldn't have gotten to where I am without the wonderful teachers I've been blessed with throughout my life.

My first instructor was Miss Alberta,

my family's cook who had worked for my mom and dad even before I was born. I had two mothers: Mimi played bridge at the club; Miss Alberta made sure I had three squares a day, something to keep me occupied, and that I stayed out of trouble. Miss Alberta was a beautiful, beautiful spirit. She indulged my endless curiosity, allowing me to play with a chemistry set in the kitchen. She trained a cautious eye on me, half expecting me to blow up the house, which she would never tolerate on her watch. Her cooking was a lot like chemistry—everything was a pinch of this, a handful of that. Nothing was measured in teaspoons. After I was grown and had gone to work for my dad at his food brokerage company, Miss Alberta came with me and made homemade lunches every day for the employees.

My father, nicknamed "Slick," had bought a house on Lake Lanier so that he could entertain clients. All through my teenage years, we spent weekends grilling steaks, burgers, and fish by the waterside. I loved taking over the fire while my father schmoozed. It was an early indication that I was born with the barbecue chip.

After my father sold his business, I decided I wanted to try my hand at pit barbecue catering. My parents thought

I was crazy. They ranked barbecue as a profession right alongside underwater basket weaving. The only person who offered any support was Miss Alberta. She introduced me to her friend Big Jim Harris, an accomplished barbecue pit master who had cooked for Jim Folsom while he served as governor of Alabama in the 1950s. Big Jim and I went into business together, and for the next eight years catered corporate events all around north Georgia. I thought I was going to do all the promoting and Big Jim all the cooking, but it transpired differently and I succumbed to the 'cue addiction. During this time, the yearning to compete on the barbecue circuit

began to stir—but I didn't act on it until many years later.

While getting the truck washed in Atlanta one day, I chatted with Janet, a lovely and charming middle school teacher. We were giddy that the Braves were headed to the World Series. I learned she had moved from up North a few years before, and I asked her out as we were watching our cars get sudsed up. I won her heart on the first date by grilling her the perfect savory, buttery steak draped in sautéed mushrooms. It was love at first bite, and we married in 1993.

After listening to me talk about competing incessantly for three or four years, Janet encouraged me to enter my first barbecue competition in Stone Mountain, Georgia, in 1996. Janet and I smoked ribs and aimed to present every one perfectly appointed to the judges. We were such greenhorns: we didn't even have a tent to cover us in case it rained. I was so nervous when the judges announced the winners, I didn't stick around to learn we'd won second place.

That first competition whetted our appetites, and we entered more contests all around the South. We soon discovered, though, that our second place at Stone Mountain was just beginner's luck. Catering skills didn't easily translate to competition. So we watched to see who consistently placed in the top tier, and we eventually approached Ed and Muriel Roith of Happy Holla BBQ—celebrated winners on the circuit and board members of the Kansas City Barbeque Society—about serving as our mentors. I don't think Ed was too keen on the idea at first, but Janet and Muriel had bonded. The Roiths allowed Janet and me to shadow them, cooking as part of their team in competitions all over the country. I would cater during the week then drive out to wherever Ed and Muriel were competing. Janet would fly or drive

to meet us after teaching all week. We were exhausted, but we watched and, most importantly, we learned.

We developed patience and trained our palates to recognize variations in flavor profiles. Through trial and error we discovered what our good food tastes like and studied how to tell in a moment whether a slice of brisket or a rib possessed the right texture to plate for the judges. Janet and I received certification in the KCBS and the Memphis Barbecue Network—the two main competition organizations—so that we could

think like judges. After two years under the Roiths' tutelage, we were able to win on our own as The Q Company. Looking back, those years with the Roiths were some of our best years in barbecue.

Soon thereafter we started racking up awards. We won the Georgia and North Carolina state championships, were named the Alabama and Nashville Fan Fair reserve grand champions, and were awarded the National Barbecue News Caterer of the Year. On winter days and for special events, Janet still wears a red cowgirl hat with five pins that note the times we've earned perfect 180 scores in KCBS-sanctioned competitions.

The most memorable of all our competitions occurred in South Carolina. Janet and I felt so confident in the food we had prepared going into the awards ceremony. Yet we sat there, sinking, as the judges called the teams for the top ten places in each of the four categories—chicken, ribs, pork, and brisket— and we were not among them. We felt so dejected we got up to leave, just as the judges named The Q Company grand champions. Even though we had placed out of the top ten in each of the four individual categories, we had earned the highest cumulative score across all categories. The South Carolina competition taught me about

the unassailable importance of consistency, and to this day it remains the single most essential value we uphold at Wiley's Championship BBQ.

Janet and I left Atlanta in 2005, finally living our dream of retiring to the southeastern coast in Savannah. I had long held the romantic notion of opening a restaurant, and we hung out our shingle in 2008 on a thirty-four-seat sliver of a space in a strip mall on Whitemarsh Island. There we cook competition barbecue for our customers every day. Our food has been road tested and road tasted. Everybody who walks through our doors is a potential judge—and with the advent of social media, a food critic.

Ask a hundred people what success is, and you will get a hundred different answers. In all my years, I've come to learn there are two kinds: internal and external. External success means getting love from a lot of other people— maybe having a bridge or road named for you, or even winning a trophy at a barbecue competition. I know how fragile that kind of success can be.

Internal success is far more satisfying and long lasting. It can come from cooking hundreds of birds for thousands of hungry people on the Day of Great Thanksgiving and asking yourself afterward, "How did I do that?" More than anything, though, it comes from honing and mastering a craft, then teaching that craft to a younger generation so that it lives on after you.

When I started catering and competing, folks stayed in places akin to the Bates Motel. We smoked chicken, ribs, brisket, and pork. Today, competitors roll up in fancy RVs and buses with entourages, and serve up pork cheeks and bellies. I shake my head sometimes and wonder where it's all going.

I recently read an article in the *National Barbecue News* about a father who organized a children's cooking competition on the circuit because he noticed more and more children traveling with their parents.

"Eventually that flame is going to die out and that page is going to turn," he wrote. "There are these kids, and teaching them the right way to [prepare barbecue] is a fantastic thing."

I couldn't agree more. For this reason alone, I teach BBQ 101 classes out of my shop. That's also why I wanted to write a cookbook. You cannot carry on a heritage if you are keeping secrets. You have got to tell those stories and eat hearty while you can, because there may not be good barbecue in heaven.

HOW TO BE A SMOKING SUCCESS

When I told a reporter at CNN that barbecue is both an art and a science, and I thought of myself as an artist, I wasn't just blowing smoke. Making barbecue requires choreography and composition. When you get all of the pieces to play in harmony, barbecue is like a symphony. Winning a competition is like getting a standing ovation at Carnegie Hall, and the only way to get there is practice, practice, practice.

To practice, you first need the right instrument. Then you need to learn how to play it. Then you need to try and fail, then fail again, only better, until you get the hang of it. Then you can improvise.

TOOLS AND EQUIPMENT

GRILLS AND SMOKERS

If Louis Armstrong gave me his trumpet, it wouldn't make me a better player. A grill or smoker should meet the cook's needs. No grill or smoker, regardless of the specifications, ever won a barbecue competition, any more than a hammer or saw built a house.

When shopping for a grill or smoker, assess how you are going to use it. Don't go straight for the Stradivarius. If you are a beginner, you may want to start with a kettle-type grill (right, top), which can be adapted for both direct heat and indirect heat—grilling and smoking. Look for sturdy legs, adjustable vents so that you can control the heat, and ash catchers for easy cleaning. The kettle is a great tool to learn the basics of grilling, and the alchemy of heat and smoke. Play with wood chips, types of charcoal, combinations of wood. When you've worn out practicing on the kettle, you've got my permission to move to the next level.

If you want quick, consistent temperature, and are willing to sacrifice a little of the charred flavor, go for a gas grill that comes with drip pans to prevent flare-ups and gas gauges so you can keep track of the tank's capacity.

If you want a dedicated smoker (below, bottom), look for one that is bullet- or barrel-shaped to allow for good heat circulation and has a water pan to maintain moisture.

UTENSILS

Barbecue mop

Basting brushes in multiple lengths and made of various materials, such as silicone

> **Tip:** You can make your own basting brushes out of woody herbs, such as thyme and rosemary.

Brushes and scrubbers to clean the grill

Disposable aluminum drip pans to capture juices for basting and to help maintain moisture

Grate grabbers

Grill baskets for fish and vegetables

Grill grates

Instant-read meat thermometers in multiple sizes

Kitchen syringes

Silicone gloves and oven mitts

Skewers for kabobs

Spatulas

Spray bottles

Tongs in various sizes

GRILLING AND SMOKING ACCESSORIES FOR CHARCOAL GRILLS

Butane lighter

Rails and side baskets

Chimney fire starter (also known as a fire chimney)

Charcoal (natural briquettes, briquettes, or lump)

A variety of wood chunks, chips, or pellets, such as pecan, applewood, cherry, walnut, hickory, oak, and mesquite

Trimmings, such as dried grapevine stems, bay, basil, or sage leaves

GRILLING AND SMOKING ACCESSORIES FOR GAS GRILLS

Drip pans

Full gas tanks, appropriate to make and model of grill

Smoker boxes

GETTING STARTED

People often confuse grilling—cooking with high, direct heat—with smoking, the low-and-slow method of producing succulent barbecue with indirect heat. Both methods require fire.

GRILLING

Grilling is simply cooking food directly over a high-heat source, whether the fire is generated by charcoal, gas, or infrared heat. It does not use smoke. You want to use the direct grilling method to sear meats to seal in their juices, and for cuts of meat that don't require long to cook, twenty minutes or so.

Always wipe your grill with olive oil when it is cool to prevent meats from sticking and for easier cleaning on the back end.

To create a fire, use charcoal—another area where you can experiment to determine your preferences. There is fierce debate in the world of grilling whether to use lump charcoal or charcoal briquettes. Lump charcoal is derived from natural woods burned until there's not much left but carbon. Briquettes are made from pressed wood by-products. Lump charcoal burns the hottest, but briquettes burn more consistently. Use a fire chimney (page 20) to start the coals. Using tongs, spread the fired coals in a single layer in the grill, then set the cooking grate on the grill. Do not cover. You're now ready to grill.

Although charcoal flavors the meat with a nice char, gas grills create heat uniformity, which prevents burning. But let me just say, if hell is any hotter than a gas grill, I most certainly don't want to go. To grill with gas, close the lid and preheat the grill on high for approximately fifteen minutes. Open the grill, then start cooking.

You can also set up your grill for indirect cooking, akin to smoking, but it's much harder to keep the temperature consistent throughout the cooking process.

To use your charcoal grill for indirect cooking, set an aluminum drip pan in the bottom center of the charcoal grate. Use the fire chimney to heat the coals, then spread them evenly on either side of the drip pan, pushing them as far to the edge as possible. Charcoal rails or holders will keep the charcoal in place. Scatter a few pieces of presoaked wood chunks, pellets, or pieces onto the hot coals to release the wood aromas. Arrange food on the cooking grid directly over the drip pan. Cover the grill and leave all the vents open. Cook according to the recipe. Replenish the charcoal every hour of cooking time.

To cook indirectly on a gas grill, preheat the grill on high for at least fifteen minutes with all of the burners on and the grill covered. Once the grill is hot, turn off one of the burners and set the meat on that burner. Set the other burner to the heat called for in the recipe. Cover the grill and cook. To impart a smoky flavor, place presoaked wood chips in a smoker box. Never throw the chips or chunks directly on a gas grill.

HOW TO USE A FiRE CHiMNEY

If you cook with charcoal, purchase a fire chimney. It will make your life easier and take less time to get the coals heated. Make sure the chimney you use has heatproof handles.

Crumple newspaper, brown paper bags, or other kindling at the bottom of the chimney. Never use the funny papers or pages with colored photographs and ads. (I'm not making any political statements here, but I've learned that the *Wall Street Journal* burns hotter than the *New York Times*.) Then fill the chimney with approximately twenty-five pieces of lump charcoal or briquettes. Grip the chimney by the handle and light the kindling using a wand lighter—without any other lighter fluids or chemicals. Place the chimney in the middle of the grill and watch for lots of smoke.

In approximately ten to fifteen minutes, the coals will be burning bright hot red. When they glow orange and grow ash gray around the edges, dump the coals in the grill and rake them into position for either direct or indirect cooking. Allow the coals to turn ashen before putting anything on the grill.

SMOKING

Whether you own a Big Green Egg or a Weber Smokey Mountain bullet, follow the directions for use.

The trick with all smoking, whether on a grill or in a dedicated smoker, is to maintain a consistent temperature throughout the cooking process. Most smokers come with a temperature gauge on the outside, but my suggestion is to have two more thermometers at your disposal—an oven thermometer attached to the inside of the smoker or grill, and a handy digital thermometer to get a read on the internal temperature of the meat.

A WORD ON WOOD

The best woods to use in barbecue come from cured, dried hardwoods. And the woods you choose can impart another subtle layer of flavor that suggests regional differences and tastes. And just like the concept of *terroir* in wine, woods are flavored by the microclimate where they are grown.

For instance, Memphis barbecue tends to favor sweet, fruitier woods, such as applewood and cherry. In places like Mississippi and Alabama, the pungent hickory is the wood of choice. Here in Georgia and South Carolina, we like to add pecan and peach. Texans prefer hickory, mesquite, and post oak—all big and bold. Take note, however, mesquite is an oily wood that can leave a thick, hard-to-clean coating on your grill grate.

Personally, I use pecan and hickory most often—but I like to experiment with different combinations. The key is to use the wood sparingly, because you can destroy a good cut of meat with too much smoke. It's meant to be an accent, not the dominant flavor. If you've ever eaten at a barbecue restaurant and belched smoke for days, you know they've used too much wood and smoke.

GRILLING AND SMOKING TEMPERATURES

People put way too much emphasis on the cooking method. Should I grill or should I smoke? The secret simply is using the method that is right for the cut of meat. You don't barbecue meat; you smoke it until it becomes barbecue.

Temperature	Method	Best Use
Low (220°F–280°F)	Indirect heat (smoking)	Large cuts, such as brisket, pork shoulder, pork butt, ribs, lamb
Medium (300°F–375°F)	Indirect heat (roasting)	Chicken, turkey, roasts
Medium-High (375°F–450°F)	Direct heat (grilling)	Steaks, burgers, fish, vegetables
High (450°F–650°F)	Direct heat	Cleaning grill grate

RECOMMENDED INTERNAL COOKING TEMPERATURES

There are all these myths out there. People will tell you there is only this way or that way to do something. Well, I'm here to tell you that a grill or a pit never won awards for making barbecue. Only cooks win awards, and the only cooks who win awards are the ones who maintain consistency in quality, texture, taste, and appearance.

The key to great barbecue is consistency, and the key to consistency is simple: *Internal temperature always prevails over time.* My biggest pet peeve is when I read cookbooks from reputable chefs and outlets that publish cooking times. I blame Betty Crocker for our loss of intuition in cooking and our embrace of standardization. Weather conditions, altitude, and cooking methods all affect time. Foods cook differently in Evergreen, Colorado, than they do in Savannah, Georgia. The air is so thin at high altitudes that it's hard to keep a fire burning. Foods also cook quicker the higher you go. I remember a competition in North Carolina when my meat was ready at 4 a.m.—hours before the judges were ready for a taste.

Therefore, always go by the internal temperature of the meat. An inexpensive digital meat thermometer (see "How to Calibrate a Meat Thermometer") will become the mightiest weapon in your barbecue arsenal. Never cut the meat to determine doneness. To test the temperature of the meat, stick the tip of the thermometer into the thickest part of the meat not next to a bone. The meat is done when it reads:

Pork butt/shoulder:	
- for pulling	190°F
- for slicing	160°F–170°F
Poultry	170°F
Fish	135°F–145°F
Beef:	
- rare	135°F–145°F
- medium	145°F–150°F
- well	150°F–165°F
Brisket	190°F

Ribs are the only meat with which you cannot use a thermometer to measure doneness. An easy way to tell if ribs have cooked thoroughly is to pick the slab up with tongs, and if they begin to "break" in the center, they are done.

When you take the meat off the heat, don't cut it immediately. Let it rest on a plate for at least ten minutes so that the juices can redistribute. Some well-done meat still will show a red or pinkish hue because of the chemical process of smoking. For this reason, always go by internal temperature to determine doneness.

HOW TO CALIBRATE A MEAT THERMOMETER

So let's repeat: *Internal temperature always prevails over time*; therefore, you need a well-calibrated thermometer to ensure that you're getting an accurate reading. Because you'll be working at moderate to high temperatures, it's best to calibrate your thermometer using the boiling water method. To do this, bring a pot of distilled water to a rolling boil. Place the thermometer probe into the boiling water for at least one minute, being careful not to let the probe touch the side or bottom of the pot. The temperature should read between 210°F and 214°F, depending on altitude. If the thermometer doesn't read within that range, adjust it to 212°F, according to manufacturer's directions.

HOW TO USE THIS COOKBOOK

Like most cookbooks, we provide a set of recipes that invite you into our kitchen for a taste. We, however, don't expect you to produce a dish exactly as we do. Although these recipes have been culled from a lifetime of cooking, catering, and competing, we encourage you to improvise, experiment, and give each recipe your own imprint. With that said, we do think certain products make a dish taste all that much better.

When a recipe calls for salt, we prefer either kosher salt or sea salt—not typical table salt, because it can impart a metallic or medicinal taste.

For Worcestershire sauce—or what I like to call "What's this here sauce?"—we use Lea & Perrins. For hot sauce, we use Cholula. For Dijon mustard, Grey Poupon. For ketchup, Hunt's or Heinz.

For honey, we like to use locally sourced brands, such as Savannah Bee Company, or one of the many brands produced by other keepers in and around Chatham County, Georgia. My favorites are orange blossom, because of the citrusy notes, and sourwood, because of the distinctive maple flavor.

When it comes to mayonnaise, there's some disagreement among our team. Janet swears by Hellmann's now, after I weaned her off the Miracle Whip her mother used back in Massachusetts. Amy, our cowriter, is an unabashed devotee of Duke's, a staple of many a Southern cupboard. I say go with what you know and like, but you might try experimenting with different versions, including a homemade version like Julia Child's or Scott Peacock's, to see how they affect the taste.

For bourbon, we try to strike a balance with inexpensive refinement. We most often turn to Evan Williams Black Label. No matter the brand, I call it "Lock-and-Key" bourbon, because we keep our bottle in a safe in the kitchen. We noticed we were buying bottles faster than we could count from the liquor store next door to the restaurant, so we started marking the level at the end of each workday. When morning came around, Janet and I noticed that the bottle was a little lighter and the liquid a little lower than when we stored it. An employee finally 'fessed up to taking a nip here and there.

Speaking of spirits, we also offer some sipping suggestions here and there, courtesy of the wine and beer experts at FORM, a gourmet wine and cheese shop here in Savannah.

GET A NOTEBOOK

Recipes are abundant, but skill and knowledge don't come from a recipe. They develop through trial, error, and practice. The Rolling Stones play a piece of music hundreds of times before they take it on the road, so that the songs become sense memory. One of the guys always ahead of us in competition early in our careers cooked everything two hundred times before he ever entered his first competition.

If a meat thermometer is the mightiest weapon in your barbecue arsenal, a plain spiral-bound notebook is your plan of attack. Even with a recipe, record what you did right, what you did wrong, where you substituted ingredients, added something new, whether or not it worked, weather conditions of the day, cooking temperatures, and final results. You may also want to note which beverages you tried and what you liked best.

The biggest lie we ever tell is the one we tell ourselves: I'll remember. So, keep a notebook at the ready.

SEASONINGS AND SPICES

Real innovation in barbecue comes by applying nuanced layers of flavor with marinades, injections, rubs, and sauces. Each layer builds upon the next, complementing but not overwhelming the taste of the meat. This stage is where you experiment and improvise to create your signature profile. Take these basic recipes and adjust the seasonings and spices to your liking, spiking them with heat or sweetness, injecting some surprise with an unusual ingredient such as Dr Pepper, sun-dried tomatoes, or pineapple juice.

MARINADES

A **marinade** *steeps the meat or vegetables in seasoned liquid, and is designed to infuse flavor as well as tenderize.*

RUBS

A **rub** *is an essential part of the barbecue process. A pungent blend of spices and seasonings cures the meat and makes a beautiful crust—or bark. It's necessary to liquefy the rubbing spices with olive or vegetable oil after you've massaged them into the meat so that they don't burn during the cooking process and leave a bitter aftertaste.*

INJECTIONS

An **injection** *gives meat a subtle yet deeper taste profile than a marinade, and provides extra moisture that can be lost during the smoking process. It is best to inject the meat before the rub, and to let the meat sit in the refrigerator overnight so that the juices have enough time to permeate the meat.*

HOW TO USE A KITCHEN INJECTOR

Slowly draw the cooled liquid into the plunger, then pierce the meat with the needle. Push the plunger into the meat and continue to press as you withdraw the needle to ensure wide distribution of the injection liquid. Repeat until all the injection liquid is used and evenly dispersed throughout the cut of meat.

Continue with a rub or other preparations. Store the meat in the refrigerator for at least three hours, but preferably overnight, until you are ready to cook it on the smoker.

SAUCES

*Woods, proteins, and **sauces** are the three pillars that define regional distinctions in barbecue. Eastern North Carolina prefers vinegar-based sauces, while western North Carolina leans toward sweet red sauces like the ones made in Kansas City. Texans use chilies to bring on the heat and honey to bring on the sweet. South Carolinians like the bite of mustard. Memphis favors thin sauces that don't compete with their dry rubs. At Wiley's, we cherish them all.*

BASIC POULTRY MARINADE

For competition, we sometimes bathe our chickens overnight in this bright, juicy blend I adapted from a recipe off the back of a jar of Grey Poupon. The marinade is designed to infuse the hens with as much succulence as possible, because chicken tends to dry out fairly fast during the smoking process. We follow with a Lemon-Pepper Rub (page 36) to give it some zing. This marinade works equally well on Cornish game hens, squab, and turkey.

MAKES 4 CUPS

> 1¹⁄₃ cups chicken broth
> 1¹⁄₃ cups high-quality, store-bought Italian salad
>   dressing, preferably Newman's Own
> 1¹⁄₃ cups prepared mustard, preferably Dijon

In a large bowl, mix the broth, dressing, and mustard until well combined.

Store the marinade in an airtight container in the refrigerator for up to 3 days, until ready to use.

Marinate chicken in a large zip-lock bag in the refrigerator overnight.

> **Tip:** Liquor stores and other bag-your-own-ice places will sell you large plastic bags that work well as marinating bags.

THE Q COMPANY'S CHICKEN MARINADE

*We took our first trophy for chicken after wallering—our word for fully immersing—
our hens in this zesty mix. We drove home all the way from South Carolina to Atlanta
with the first-place trophy attached to the front of our truck with a bungee cord, like it
was a hood ornament.*

MAKES 2 CUPS

$1/2$ cup freshly squeezed orange juice

$1/4$ cup freshly squeezed lemon juice

$1/4$ cup chopped fresh parsley

3 cloves garlic, peeled and minced

1 tablespoon finely chopped fresh rosemary

1 tablespoon dried oregano

1 tablespoon kosher salt

1 tablespoon freshly cracked Tellicherry black peppercorns

1 tablespoon Dijon mustard

1 tablespoon Worcestershire sauce

$1/4$ cup extra virgin olive oil

In a large bowl, thoroughly combine the juices, parsley, garlic, rosemary, oregano, salt, black pepper, mustard, and Worcestershire sauce.

Whisk in the olive oil slowly to create an emulsion. Taste and adjust salt and pepper as necessary. It's okay if this marinade is a little on the salty side.

Store the marinade in an airtight container in the refrigerator for up to 3 days, until ready to use.

Marinate chicken breasts in a plastic bag in the refrigerator overnight.

APRICOT MARINADE

This versatile marinade draws out the best in just about any meat, saturating it with a lightly sweet peachiness. Marinate fish for ¹/₂ hour, pork for at least 6 hours, and poultry for at least 3 hours.

MAKES 3 CUPS

> ¹/₂ cup diced dried apricots
>
> 1 cup dry white wine, such as a Sauvignon Blanc or Pinot Gris
>
> 2 tablespoons Dijon mustard
>
> ¹/₂ cup white wine vinegar
>
> ²/₃ cup canola oil
>
> 1 tablespoon sea salt
>
> 1 teaspoon coarsely ground black pepper

In a heavy-bottomed saucepan over medium heat, simmer the apricots in the wine for 30 minutes, until the apricots have begun to dissolve. Set aside to cool.

In a blender or food processor, puree the apricot mixture with the mustard and vinegar until smooth. While keeping the processor on low speed, drizzle in the oil then sprinkle in salt and pepper.

Store in an airtight container in the refrigerator for up to 3 days, until ready to use.

MOJO SAUCE

Maybe it's because we live in such a temperate climate that I am drawn to marinades and sauces with lots of citrus, especially a traditional mojo sauce from the Caribbean like this one. These sauces are great for both fish and fowl—and even vegetables. You can buy any number of good sauces right off the shelf, but they are ridiculously easy to prepare, taste best fresh, and invite improvisation. Don't have sour oranges? Use grapefruit.

A word of caution: when preparing seafood, don't let it sit in the sauce for longer than 20 minutes or the acid will "cook" the fish and you'll have ceviche instead.

MAKES 1^1/$_2$ CUPS

> ^{1}/$_2$ cup olive oil
> 1 whole garlic, cloves peeled and smashed
> 1 jalapeño pepper, seeded and thinly sliced
> ^{1}/$_2$ cup freshly squeezed orange juice
> ^{1}/$_4$ cup freshly squeezed lemon juice
> ^{1}/$_4$ cup freshly squeezed lime juice
> 1^1/$_2$ teaspoons dried oregano
> ^{1}/$_4$ teaspoon kosher salt
> ^{1}/$_4$ teaspoon freshly ground black pepper

Heat the oil in a medium saucepan over high heat, then add the garlic. Shake the pan until the garlic begins to turn golden around the edges.

Remove the pan from the heat and add the remaining ingredients. Stir until well combined, then set the sauce aside to cool.

Once cooled, you can marinate your protein of choice.

LAMB MARINADE

Lamb's taste and texture grows decidedly more sharp and unctuous as it ages. Pink-fleshed spring lamb has a mild, silky taste, while a juvenile lamb's flavor has a bit more tang and edge. To add a savory note, steep a shank, a rack, or chops in this garlicky, Mediterranean-inspired marinade for at least 6 and up to 24 hours.

MAKES 1 CUP

$1/2$ cup olive oil
$1/4$ cup freshly squeezed lemon juice
4 cloves garlic, minced
1 tablespoon dried oregano
2 teaspoons coarse sea salt
1 teaspoon freshly ground black pepper

In a small bowl, combine the olive oil, lemon juice, garlic, oregano, salt, and pepper.

Store in an airtight container in the refrigerator for up to 3 days.

THE Q COMPANY'S BASIC RUB

The secret to a good bark (with a bite)—that crisp crust atop a brisket, butt, or shoulder—starts with a generous massage of a pungent, smoky rub that caramelizes and deepens during the low-and-slow smoking process.

MAKES 3 CUPS

> 1 cup granulated sugar
> 1/2 cup Hungarian paprika
> 1/4 cup seasoning salt
> 1/4 cup granulated garlic
> 1/4 cup onion salt
> 1/4 cup celery salt
> 1/4 cup chili powder
> 1/4 cup black pepper
> 1 teaspoon ground dry mustard
> 1/2 teaspoon cayenne pepper

Combine all the ingredients in an airtight container and shake vigorously until thoroughly mixed.

Store in a dry, cool place for up to 6 months, until ready to use.

> **Tip:** Adapt this basic rub to suit your tastes. For a more intense caramel flavor, substitute turbinado or brown sugar, one to one, for the granulated sugar in the recipe. Experiment by adding different brands of dry mustards. Vary the types of chili powders, using a smoky ancho, for example. Throw in some oregano or thyme.

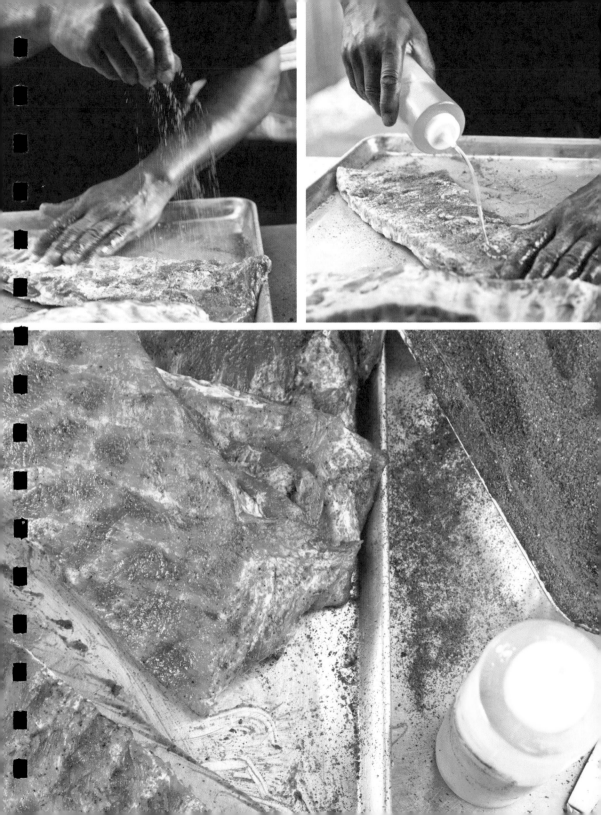

LEMON-PEPPER RUB

Sure, you can buy lemon-pepper seasoning at the grocery store. But cracking or grinding your own peppercorns delivers more zing to a dish. The sharpness of the pepper is balanced by the intense tartness of the lemon, both of which mellow during the cooking. I use this rub on chicken and as a complement to The Q Company's Basic Rub (page 34) on pulled pork and ribs.

MAKES 1⅓ CUPS

> 1 cup whole black peppercorns
> ⅓ cup dried lemon peel

Coarsely grind the peppercorns in a clean spice or coffee grinder.

Combine the ground peppercorns and lemon peel in a clean jar with a lid. Close the lid and shake the spices until well combined.

Store in an airtight container in a dry, cool place for up to 6 months.

> **Tip:** Add dried onion and thyme or granulated garlic powder for even more flavor.

GARLIC-PEPPER RUB

The amount of garlic in this recipe should cure any ills you have and keep vampires at bay. It will also draw out the best flavor in any protein: beef, pork, chicken, or fish. Go for broke on pork butt or ribs. Chicken and fish, however, can be overseasoned, so use judiciously. It works well alone or in conjunction with other marinades and rubs.

MAKES 3 CUPS

> 1¼ cups granulated garlic
> 1 cup freshly ground black pepper
> ½ cup sea salt
> ¼ cup granulated sugar
> 1 tablespoon granulated onion
> 1 tablespoon dried parsley

Combine all the ingredients in an airtight container and shake vigorously until thoroughly mixed.

Store in a dry, cool place for up to 6 months, until ready to use.

CAJUN RUB

Turkey, even smoked, can taste bland without some added seasonings. This savory blend, given to us by our good friend Bill Green, permeates the flesh and imparts an aftertaste of restrained heat. Use it sparingly on chicken, duck, and other poultry.

MAKES 3$^1/_2$ CUPS

    1 cup dried thyme
    1 cup paprika
    $^1/_3$ cup coarse sea salt
    $^1/_3$ cup garlic powder
    $^1/_3$ cup onion powder
    $^1/_3$ cup crushed red pepper
    $^1/_3$ cup freshly ground black pepper

Combine all the ingredients in an airtight container and shake vigorously until thoroughly mixed.

Store in a dry, cool place for up to 6 months, until ready to use.

LAMB RUB

For a long time we used this Lamb Rub only on lamb. Then one day we ran out of The Q Company's Basic Rub (page 34) and used the Lamb Rub on some prime rib. Then we rubbed it all over some tri-tip. We didn't realize it was so versatile.

MAKES ¼ CUP

> 1½ teaspoons dried thyme
> 1½ teaspoons dried basil
> 1½ teaspoons dried rosemary
> 1½ teaspoons granulated garlic
> 1 teaspoon sea salt
> 1 teaspoon paprika
> 1 teaspoon coarsely ground black pepper
> ¾ teaspoon ground cumin

Combine all the ingredients in an airtight container and shake vigorously until thoroughly mixed.

Store in a dry, cool place for up to 6 months, until ready to use.

THE Q COMPANY'S PORK INJECTION

Use this salty-sweet injection to introduce a deep, subtle complexity to the flavor of pulled pork. It provides the rhythmic bass line—or bottom—to the improvisational blues that is barbecue.

MAKES 3 CUPS

> 2 cups water
> 1/4 cup granulated sugar
> 3 tablespoons dry sherry
> 2 tablespoons orange blossom honey
> 2 tablespoons Grade A medium amber maple syrup
> 1 tablespoon Worcestershire sauce
> 1 tablespoon soy sauce
> 1 teaspoon granulated garlic
> 1 teaspoon kosher salt

Combine all the ingredients in a heavy-bottomed saucepan over medium-high heat. Bring the mixture to a boil, stirring constantly until all the sugar is dissolved.

Set the injection mixture aside to cool. Store in an airtight container in the refrigerator for up to 2 weeks, until ready to use.

WILEY'S RIB SPRAY

Ribs tend to lose valuable moisture during the smoking process. One way to maintain the toothsome tenderness so close to the bone is by lightly spraying the racks each time you turn them over. This spray also keeps the bark on a butt or brisket from burning, while adding just a kiss of sweetness.

MAKES 1 CUP

> 1/3 cup apple cider vinegar
> 1/3 cup apple juice
> 1/3 cup water
> Worcestershire sauce

Combine all the ingredients in a spray bottle and shake vigorously, adding 1 teaspoon Worcestershire sauce at a time to darken the mixture to your liking, while being careful not to overpower it with flavor. (Don't forget to write down in your notebook how many teaspoons you added so that you won't forget.)

Store the spray in the refrigerator for up to 1 week, until ready to use.

BARBECUE ETIQUETTE

The flavor of the meat should dominate. Rubs, marinades, and sauces all are meant to complement the natural essence of whatever protein you are grilling or smoking. Always serve sauce on the side.

When eating barbecue, always taste the meat, then the sauce, then the meat and the sauce together. Never dump the sauce all over the meat without tasting it first. You can always tell a barbecue rookie: I had a customer, who wasn't fond of reading labels, empty half a bottle of pepper sauce on his pulled pork. His mouth was on fire after he took one bite. Janet offered to get him a new sandwich.

THE Q COMPANY'S BASIC BBQ SAUCE

Over the years, we've experimented with any number of sauces—some with jaw-clenching tartness, others with honeyed sweetness. We worked with our mentors Ed and Muriel Roith to arrive at our basic sauce—a balanced tomato-based sauce that any Kansas City Barbeque Society member would appreciate. We mix it with Savannah Bee Company honey for basting and for that final shellacking before we send our meats out to be judged.

MAKES 6 1/2 CUPS

> 5 cups (40 ounces) prepared ketchup
> 1 cup light brown sugar
> 2/3 cup dark amber maple syrup
> 1 tablespoon apple cider vinegar
> 1 tablespoon molasses
> 1 tablespoon granulated garlic
> 1 tablespoon chili powder
> 1 tablespoon dry mustard
> 1 tablespoon hot sauce
> 1 scant teaspoon Worcestershire sauce
> 1/2 teaspoon ground cumin
> 1/2 teaspoon celery salt

Combine all the ingredients in a medium, nonreactive saucepan over low heat. Stir occasionally as it simmers for at least 20 minutes.

Set aside to cool to room temperature. You may use it immediately, or store it in an airtight container in the refrigerator for up to 3 months.

We encourage you to play with this sauce's notes. For a sweeter sauce, substitute honey for molasses in the recipe. For a sauce that packs more tingle, throw in some crushed red pepper flakes. For a smokier sauce, add

(continued)

ground ancho chili powder. The point, dear readers, is to make it to suit your own tastes.

Tip: You can use the barbecue sauce as a base for any number of other sauces and dips just by adding a few more ingredients. Using 1 cup of barbecue sauce as a foundation, you can make . . .

Vegetable dip, by adding 2 cups mayonnaise and 1/4 cup freshly grated Parmesan cheese.

French dressing, by adding ¾ cup olive oil and 1 tablespoon granulated garlic. Transform this condiment into a poppy seed dressing by stirring in ¼ cup poppy seeds.

Sweet and sour sauce, by adding 1 cup honey and ¼ cup low-sodium soy sauce.

Honey mustard dipping sauce, by adding ¼ cup mustard and ¼ cup honey.

Hot wing sauce, by adding ¼ cup melted butter and ½ teaspoon cayenne pepper.

WHAT'S ALL THE BUZZ ABOUT?

"I can't think of barbecue sauce without thinking of my grandfather's recipe. His secret ingredient? Honey. That's probably why Wiley's is my favorite barbecue in Savannah."
—Ted Dennard, Founder, Savannah Bee Company

Savannah is peppered with people who've turned their passions into profits—artists, designers, soap makers, tech start-ups, scratch bakers. I'm drawn to these kindred spirits who've mortgaged security for possibility. One of these passioneers, Ted Dennard, the founder of Savannah Bee Company, is one of our regulars and a neighbor. He lives on Wilmington Island, not far from the shop, and his base of operation sits a few miles east, on Johnny Mercer Boulevard.

Ted literally got stung by the beekeeping bug at age twelve, and without any grand business plan, he's grown what was a hobby into a lifelong mission. Sound familiar?

Ted travels the world, teaching sustainable beekeeping methods and sourcing. But he always returns to his native Savannah, where he sells superior-quality honeys, including one especially formulated for the grill. It's a real treat to go into his downtown storefront to sample a flight of honeys. Even better to cook with them.

BIG JIM'S BEER BBQ SAUCE

Big Jim Harris, my partner for the first eight years of catering, came by his name honestly. He stood 6 feet 3 inches tall and weighed around 250 pounds. He drove around in a big van and had a personality as outsized as his shoe size. The only thing he loved more than women was cooking barbecue—and he was a master at it. He gave me this tried-and-true recipe for basting chicken and ribs.

MAKES 6$^1/_2$ CUPS

> 2 cups (16-ounce can) beer, preferably a Pabst Blue Ribbon tall boy
>
> 2 cups ketchup
>
> 1 cup apple cider vinegar
>
> $^2/_3$ cup firmly packed dark brown sugar
>
> $^1/_3$ cup Worcestershire sauce
>
> 2 teaspoons paprika
>
> 2 teaspoons dry mustard
>
> 1 teaspoon chili powder
>
> 1 teaspoon salt
>
> 2 medium onions, thinly sliced
>
> 1 lemon, thinly sliced and seeds removed

In a medium saucepan, combine all the ingredients except the onions and lemon and bring to a boil over medium-high heat, stirring constantly.

Reduce the heat to medium and cook uncovered for 5 minutes.

Add the onions and lemon, then heat through.

WILEY'S NORTH CAROLINA SAUCE

I prefer a North Carolina–style vinegar-based sauce on my pork, and have often used Chez John's Fat Johnny's Bastardized Piedmont Sauce recipe, which you can find all over the Internet. I've also turned to Kate's Mountain Vinegar Sauce out of Steven Raichlen's BBQ USA cookbook. One day I combined elements of the two to come up with my own signature sauce with just the right amount of tartness and heat.

MAKES 2 QUARTS

4 cups apple cider vinegar

2 (12-ounce) bottles prepared barbecue sauce, such as Head Country Original BBQ Sauce

1 cup firmly packed dark brown sugar

1/4 cup granulated sugar

2 tablespoons sea salt

2 tablespoons Worcestershire sauce

1 tablespoon crushed red pepper flakes

1 teaspoon celery salt

1 teaspoon dry mustard

1 teaspoon black pepper

Combine all the ingredients in a large, nonreactive stockpot over medium-high heat. Stir until well combined and bring to a boil.

Reduce the heat to low and simmer for 10 to 15 minutes until all the sugars and salts have dissolved completely. Remove the pan from the heat and let cool.

Store in an airtight container in the refrigerator for up to 3 weeks, until you're ready to tart up a pulled pork sandwich.

WILEY'S SOUTH CAROLINA SAUCE

If you've ever stopped at a roadside barbecue stand and been served a sauce on your ribs that's yellow instead of red, you were probably in South Carolina. The Palmetto State is known for its piquant mustard-based sauces, which is great for pork and beef, but can sometimes overpower chicken. But mix a little honey with it and you've got a great dipping sauce.

MAKES 6 CUPS

> 4 cups prepared mustard
> 2 cups mayonnaise
> 1 cup water
> ³⁄₄ cup ketchup
> 8 tablespoons (1 stick) unsalted butter
> 4 tablespoons granulated or light brown sugar
> 4 tablespoons Worcestershire sauce
> 1 tablespoon salt
> 1 tablespoon freshly ground black pepper
> 1 teaspoon Kitchen Bouquet Browning and Seasoning Sauce

Combine all the ingredients in a large, nonreactive stockpot over medium-high heat. Stir until well combined and bring to a boil.

Reduce the heat to low and simmer for 20 minutes, until you have a thick, golden sauce. If it's not pourable, add a little more mustard and water. Taste and adjust seasonings and sweetness as necessary.

Remove the pan from the heat and let the sauce cool. Store in an airtight container in the refrigerator for up to 3 weeks, until you're ready to slather some good-sized beef ribs.

TEXAS OUTBACK BBQ SAUCE

When we were on the circuit, we often competed against (and made friends with) a great team called the Texas Outback Cookers, led by Ed Mullen. Ed eventually moved to North Carolina and is no longer competing. Yet, like the fine mentor he is, he shared his sauce recipe with us.

MAKES 3½ CUPS

> 4 tablespoons (½ stick) unsalted butter
> 1½ cups red wine or apple cider vinegar
> ¾ cup (6 ounces) tomato sauce
> ½ cup Worcestershire sauce
> 2 tablespoons ketchup
> 1 tablespoon dark brown sugar
> 2 teaspoons liquid smoke
> 2 teaspoons seasoning salt
> 2 teaspoons minced garlic
> 2 teaspoons paprika
> 1 teaspoon Tabasco sauce
> ½ teaspoon freshly ground black pepper
> ¼ teaspoon ground cayenne pepper

In a medium saucepan, melt the butter over low heat. Once the butter has melted, stir in the vinegar, tomato sauce, Worcestershire sauce, and ketchup.

Let the sauce heat a bit, then add the sugar, liquid smoke, salt, garlic, paprika, Tabasco sauce, and peppers. Bring the sauce to a boil, then lower the heat and simmer for 15 minutes, stirring occasionally and making sure the sugar dissolves completely.

Set the sauce aside to cool. Store in an airtight container in the refrigerator for up to 3 weeks, until ready to use for basting, as a sauce, or both.

* SMOKE HOUSE CLUB w/ff 11 95

* fried Green tomatoes 5 00

* Smoked Corn on the Cob 2 75

COW AND LAMB

Rick Kaplan, president of CNN at the time, hired us to cater the millennium celebration at the network's headquarters. We turned the lobby of CNN's storied tower into a barbecue joint, serving ribs and pulled pork all night while reporters rushed about discussing Y2K hysteria and the celebrations happening all around the world. (I learned that day that Wolf Blitzer really likes hot dogs.) During the course of the evening, Rick and I gabbed for a long time, and he grew intrigued by the competition barbecue subculture. He asked if he could send his camera crew along to film us at an upcoming contest, and we said, "C'mon!"

Reporter Bruce Burkhardt and his cameraman rode along with us in the RV up to Nashville, Tennessee. On the drive, Janet made a comment about my wanting to be the Colonel Sanders of the barbecue world, and I said, "Colonel, hell! I want to be the general." My nickname was born in that moment. We won in brisket that weekend with a perfect score of 180, and it was all captured on a CNN special report.

When we were researching menu options for our restaurant, many people told us to not even bother with beef. Only people out West eat beef, they said, and people in Georgia only want pig. I'm glad we didn't listen. Brisket ranks No. 2 in sales in our little shop, and we are one of the few restaurants in Savannah to serve it. Our Friday special, the Smoked Corned Beef Reuben (page 56), is a huge hit, as is the Smokehouse Meatloaf (page 70) on Wednesdays. Both dishes are typical diner fare raised to a much higher level of taste by virtue of barbecue.

THE Q COMPANY'S BRISKET

When cooking brisket, leave as much of the fat on as you can during the cooking process. Otherwise—no fat, no flavor. Most of it will melt away, then you can trim whatever fat remains when you are ready to serve.

SERVES 6 TO 8

> 1 (5- to 6-pound) beef brisket
> 1 cup The Q Company's Basic Rub (page 34)
> 1/4 cup Garlic-Pepper Rub (page 37)
> Olive oil

Wash the brisket under cold running water, then pat dry. Massage the Basic Rub into the meat, covering every surface and getting into all the nooks and crannies. Repeat with the Garlic-Pepper Rub, then the olive oil.

Cover the brisket in plastic wrap and chill inside the refrigerator for 5 to 8 hours, preferably overnight.

Bring your smoker up to between 225°F and 240°F. Remove the brisket from the refrigerator, unwrap it, and place the brisket, fat side up, in a shallow aluminum pan. Set the pan in the middle of the rack. Cover the smoker and let the brisket smoke for 5 to 8 hours, depending on its size. Occasionally baste the brisket with its own juices or spritz with Wiley's Rib Spray (page 41).

When the brisket has reached an internal temperature of 190°F in the thickest part of the meat, remove the pan from the grill and set it aside for 10 to 15 minutes so that the brisket's juices reconstitute.

Transfer the brisket to a cutting surface and slice it against the grain, about 1/4 inch thick.

(continued)

When plating, put the fat cap on bottom and the bark on top, then pour the remaining juices in the pan over the slices. Serve immediately.

> **Tip:** You must cut brisket against the grain or it will be tough and stringy. Sometimes, though, it is hard to tell exactly where the grain is after you have smoked the meat. Before you apply the rub, cut off one of the corners so you know which way the grain runs.
>
> Don't throw those tips away—smoke them too!

BURNT ENDS
A real delicacy.

After you take the brisket from the smoker and you've let the juices reconstitute, cut the point muscle from the whole brisket and make this little delicacy by spraying the point with Wiley's Rib Spray (page 41), then smoking for another $1/2$ hour. Flip, spray, and smoke another $1/2$ hour. Repeat for another hour.

When the point is slightly crisp all over the outside, but still juicy on the inside, remove the point from the smoker, chop it into cubes, toss it with some sauce spiked with a little honey, then serve with a couple of slices of buttered Texas toast.

WRAP TWO WAYS
Perfect for leftovers.

BRISKET WRAP

       1 (12-inch) flour tortilla
       5 ounces The Q Company's Brisket (page 52), sliced

2 ounces shredded lettuce

2 ounces grated white cheddar cheese

$1/2$ ounce sliced and sautéed onions and green peppers

1 tablespoon unsalted butter, melted

Open the tortilla flat and layer the brisket, lettuce, cheese, onions, and peppers in the center. Fold the tortilla edges over until the contents are tightly wrapped, then brush the tortilla with melted butter.

On a heated waffle iron, George Foreman Grill, or panini maker, press the wrap until it's golden brown. Serve immediately.

BLACK AND BLUE WRAP

2 tablespoons butter

$1/2$ medium Vidalia onion, sliced

$1/2$ medium green bell pepper, seeded and sliced

$1/2$ medium yellow bell pepper, seeded and sliced

1 to 2 tablespoons Wiley's Special Mushrooms (page 62)

1 (10-inch) spinach flatbread wrap

Blue cheese dressing

5 ounces The Q Company's Brisket (page 52), sliced

In a cast-iron skillet over medium heat, melt the butter, then add the onion and peppers. Sauté the onion and peppers until they are soft and caramelized, approximately 10 to 13 minutes.

Lay the spinach wrap flat and slather with blue cheese dressing. Layer the brisket, grilled onions, peppers, and mushrooms in the center. Fold the wrap edges over until the contents are tightly wrapped. Serve immediately.

SMOKED CORNED BEEF REUBEN

Our Friday lunch special, born from a St. Patrick's Day celebration, has become my favorite sandwich. I didn't even know I liked sauerkraut until I tried it. And many a person who previously disliked corned beef has become a fan after one bite, owing to the intense flavor drawn out from slow smoking.

SERVES 10

> 1 (5-pound) corned beef brisket, sliced
> 20 slices Texas toast
> Thousand Island dressing
> 40 slices Swiss cheese
> 1 jar (32 ounces) sauerkraut

Bring the smoker up to 225°F, place the corned beef on the smoker plate, and cover the smoker. Smoke the corned beef until it reaches an internal temperature of 190°F, approximately 6 hours.

Once the corned beef has reached the desired temperature, remove it from the smoker and let it rest at least 15 minutes for the juices to reconstitute. Slice it against the grain, about ¼ inch thick.

Slather one side of the toast with Thousand Island dressing, then place a slice of Swiss cheese on each piece of toast. On half the slices, place 4 tablespoons sauerkraut, then several slices of corned beef.

Put the sandwiches together, then press in a panini maker for 3 to 4 minutes, until the toast is golden and crispy. Serve immediately.

SAVANNAH'S ST. PATRICK'S DAY CELEBRATION

When Janet and I first moved to Savannah, we rented a Victorian home in the Historic Landmark District on one of the squares. There, we experienced our first St. Patrick's Day Festival together. This may not sound like much to the uninitiated, but every March about 400,000 visitors descend upon the Hostess City in what is reportedly the country's second biggest St. Patrick's Day celebration. Now, I don't know about the accuracy of that number, but it does feel like every amateur drinker this side of the Mississippi heads our way.

Back in those days before we opened the restaurant, we would get up early, stake our claim on a curb on the parade route, then watch as crazed women jumped out of the crowd and kissed every man marching in uniform. We'd also witness thousands of people getting soaked with green beer and green grits. I used to stay up past midnight, but I can't do that anymore.

Now we enjoy the celebration from the quiet confines of Whitemarsh Island, where we await a late rush of happily drunk patrons hungry for smoked corned beef.

HONKY TONK SANDWICH

On the rare occasion we found ourselves with leftover corned beef on a Saturday, we concocted this spicy and savory sandwich as an alternative to the traditional Reuben. Well, the Honky Tonk was such a hit, we made it a weekend special.

SERVES 10

>   1 (5-pound) corned beef brisket
>   10 croissants
> $^{1}/_{2}$ cup mayonnaise
>   10 slices pepper Jack cheese
>   10 slices Swiss cheese
>   6 cups fresh spinach, sautéed in garlic and olive oil
>   1 (26-ounce) can pickled and sliced jalapeño
>   peppers, drained (optional)

Bring the smoker up to 225°F, place the corned beef on the smoker plate, and cover. Smoke the corned beef until it reaches an internal temperature of 190°F, approximately 6 hours.

Once the corned beef has reached the desired temperature, remove it from the smoker and let it rest at least 15 minutes for the juices to reconstitute. Slice it against the grain, about $^{1}/_{4}$ inch thick.

Butterfly slice the croissants and open them to build your sandwiches. Slather the croissants with mayonnaise. Lay a slice of pepper Jack cheese on one side and a slice of Swiss cheese on the other. Place one-tenth of the spinach on one side, a few jalapeño peppers on the other. Top with several slices of corned beef.

Close the croissants, then press them in a panini maker for 3 to 4 minutes, until golden and crispy. Serve immediately.

PERFECT STEAK WITH WILEY'S SPECIAL MUSHROOMS

The rib-eye, sometimes called the Delmonico, comes from the small end of a rib roast. It's swirled with lots of marbling, which translates into great taste. While grilling, keep an open can of beer close by to extinguish any flare-ups caused by the fat. The beer puts out the fire, gives off a heady aroma, and leaves behind a rich flavor.

SERVES 4

> 1 cup teriyaki sauce
> 1 cup red wine vinegar
> 1 cup water
> $1/4$ cup good-quality Kentucky bourbon
> 4 boneless rib-eye steaks, at least $1^1/2$ inches thick
> Wiley's Special Mushrooms (page 62)

In a medium bowl, mix together the teriyaki sauce, red wine vinegar, water, and bourbon. Transfer the marinade to a heavy-duty plastic bag with a secure enclosure.

Wash the steaks under cold running water, then pat the steaks dry. Place them in the marinade and close the bag. Allow the meat to marinate at least 3 hours, but preferably overnight.

Prepare the grill for high heat.

Remove the steaks from the marinade. Rinse the steaks and pat them dry. Lay the steaks diagonally across the grill grates in order to get good marks. Turn the steaks after 4 minutes. After another 4 minutes, flip the steaks again. Monitor the temperature of the steaks with a thermometer through the thickest part. Do not take the reading immediately after turning, as you will get a higher and inaccurate reading.

(continued)

When the steaks have reached the desired internal temperature (see "Internal Temperature for Steaks" below), remove them from the grill and let them rest for at least 10 minutes to allow the meat's juices to reconstitute.

Plate the steaks, then spoon Wiley's Special Mushrooms over the top. Serve immediately.

INTERNAL TEMPERATURE FOR STEAKS

Rare = 125°F–130°F

Medium = 135°F–140°F

Well = 140°F–150°F

Sacrificed = 151°F plus

WILEY'S SPECIAL MUSHROOMS

Goes with everything.

SERVES 4

2 tablespoons butter
1 pint cleaned, stemmed, and sliced white mushrooms
2 teaspoons seasoning salt
Splash Worcestershire sauce

In a large skillet over medium heat, melt the butter, then add the mushrooms. Do not crowd the mushrooms. Sprinkle the mushrooms with seasoning salt, then add the Worcestershire sauce. Sauté the mushrooms until they are evenly coated and turn brown. Spoon over each steak.

SMOKED BEEF TENDERLOIN WITH ROQUEFORT SAUCE

When Janet and I got married twenty years ago on the banks of the Chattahoochee River, we each had a signature dish. I chose this succulent tenderloin as mine, and paired it with a Roquefort Sauce from a 1985 recipe book Janet brought with her from Massachusetts—the Sconset Café *cookbook by Pamela McKinstry. We make this dish for special occasions, and it's always served on our sideboard on Christmas Eve.*

SERVES 6

> $^1/_3$ cup low-sodium teriyaki sauce
> $^1/_3$ cup water
> $^1/_4$ cup good-quality Kentucky bourbon
> 1 (3- to 4-pound) trimmed beef tenderloin
> $^1/_4$ cup coarsely ground black pepper
> $^1/_4$ cup coarse sea salt
> $^1/_4$ granulated garlic
> Olive oil
> Roquefort Sauce (page 65)

In a medium bowl, mix together the teriyaki sauce, water, and bourbon. Transfer the marinade to a heavy-duty plastic bag with a secure enclosure.

Wash the tenderloin under cold running water, then pat the tenderloin dry. Place the tenderloin in the marinade and close the bag. Allow the meat to marinate at least 3 hours, but preferably overnight.

In a small bowl, mix the black pepper, sea salt, and garlic together for a savory rub. Remove the tenderloin from the marinade and rinse it under cold running water. Pat the tenderloin dry, and then massage it with the dry rub. Liquefy the rub ingredients with the olive oil.

(continued)

Bring the smoker up to between 220°F and 240°F. Smoke the tenderloin until the internal temperature reaches 135°F to 145°F.

Remove the tenderloin from the smoker and let it rest for at least 10 minutes to allow the meat's juices to reconstitute. When you are ready to serve, slice the tenderloin against the grain in 6- to 8-ounce slices. Serve immediately with a side of Roquefort Sauce.

Tip: If you buy a whole beef tenderloin roast, also known as a Chateaubriand, you'll want to make sure the silver skin—that thick, opaque, white connective tissue with a silvery sheen—has been removed, if not by the butcher, then by yourself.

To remove the silver skin, lay the cold tenderloin roast pointing away from you. (It's always easier to cut raw meat when it's cold.) Beginning at an outer edge of the silver skin, make a ¼-inch incision just beneath the skin with a sharp boning knife and begin to slice the skin away from you as you pull the skin up and away. Try to keep the knife blade flat against the muscle surface so that you don't lose any precious meat. Once you get that ¼-inch strip removed, repeat the process until all of the silver skin has been excised.

Turn the tenderloin over and trim any excess fat. You can prepare the tenderloin at this point as a whole roast, or you can cut the loin into 6- to 8-ounce fillets.

ROQUEFORT SAUCE

Rich and decadent.

MAKES 2 TO 3 CUPS

  1 quart heavy cream
  1 cup cognac
  $^2/_3$ cup beef stock
  $1^1/_4$ cups (18 ounces) Roquefort cheese crumbles,
    or other good-quality French blue cheese
  1 ($3^1/_2$-ounce) jar green peppercorns
  Salt and black pepper

In a heavy-bottomed saucepan, combine the cream, cognac, and stock. Whisking constantly over medium heat, reduce the cream mixture until it is thick like gravy, approximately 15 to 20 minutes. Stir in the cheese and whisk until the cheese is completely melted and the sauce is smooth.

Crush the peppercorns with the back of a cast-iron skillet, then sprinkle into the sauce. Taste the sauce to determine whether it needs any salt or pepper for taste.

Spoon the sauce over the beef tenderloins or serve it on the side in a silver gravy boat.

> **Sipping Suggestion:** The richer and more flavorful the cut of beef, so too should the beer be! Try a full, smoky chicory or chocolate stout. And although you may tend toward a velvety Cabernet Sauvignon, don't negate a peppery Cabernet Franc or an earthy Merlot from Washington State. A Bordeaux, such as Saint-Émilion, pairs nicely as well.

TRI-TIP

An oft-overlooked piece of meat, the beef tri-tip typically weighs between 1½ and 2½ pounds. It comes from the bottom of the sirloin cut and is shaped like a triangle. It had been relegated to stew meat and lean ground hamburger until some butchers in California started to recommend it to customers for grilling. Thinly sliced tri-tip works well in wraps, on top of sautéed spinach, or layered across a bed of mixed greens.

SERVES 4

> 1 (4-pound) tri-tip, marinated
> ¼ cup kosher salt
> ¼ cup coarsely ground black pepper
> 4 tablespoons Garlic-Pepper Rub (page 37)
> 4 tablespoons Lamb Rub (page 39)
> Olive oil

Rinse the tri-tip under cold running water, then pat dry. Trim the fat and membrane from the meat.

Rub the meat with salt, followed by black pepper, Garlic-Pepper Rub, then the Lamb Rub. Massage the seasonings on all sides, then liquefy the seasonings with olive oil.

Prepare the grill for medium-high heat. Place the tri-tip on the grill grate directly over the heat and let the meat grill for 20 minutes. Flip the meat over and grill for 20 minutes more.

Test the meat's internal temperature and pull the meat off the grill when it reaches the desired level of doneness, according to the chart on page 62. Let the meat rest up to 10 minutes before serving.

SMOKED PRIME RIB WITH AU JUS

Considering Saturday night is often date night for a lot of couples, we thought we'd fancy it up and offer a nice cut for our dinner special. People line up to get it, and we often run out. So the regulars who have wised up call ahead and reserve some for pickup. We like to serve this dish with sides of Grilled Asparagus (page 173) and Twice-Baked Potatoes (page 152).

SERVES 10 TO 12

> 1 (10-pound) prime rib roast
> Kosher salt
> Coarsely ground black pepper
> 1 cup Lamb Rub (page 39)
> Several sprigs fresh rosemary, leaves
>   removed and coarsely chopped
> Olive oil
> Au Jus (page 69)

Rinse the prime rib roast under cold running water, then pat dry.

Rub the roast on all sides with seasonings to taste, first with salt, then pepper, then Lamb Rub, and finally rosemary leaves. Liquefy the seasonings with olive oil.

Bring the smoker up to 225°F. Place the roast in the smoker, cover the smoker, and smoke until the roast reaches an internal temperature of 155°F—the perfect medium rare.

Cover the roast with aluminum foil and hold until serving. Let it rest at least 15 minutes to allow the juices to reconstitute. Serve with a side of prepared horseradish sauce or Au Jus.

AU JUS

Nice and savory.

 4 cups beef broth
 4 cups water
 2 tablespoons Better Than Bouillon Beef Base
 2 teaspoons black pepper
 10 bay leaves

Combine all the ingredients in a stockpot and bring to a boil over medium-high heat, stirring occasionally. Turn the heat to low and simmer 20 minutes. Remove the bay leaves before serving.

FRENCH DIP SANDWICH

Mais oui *on Mondays.*

SERVES 4

 Prepared horseradish sauce
 4 (6-inch) Cuban rolls, sliced open
 1 pound prime rib roast, sliced
 1 green, yellow, or red bell pepper, sautéed
 2 cups sliced mushrooms, sautéed
 1 cup shredded Swiss cheese
 2 cups Au Jus (above), warmed

To assemble each sandwich, slather horseradish sauce on the inside of Cuban rolls. Layer one-fourth of the prime rib slices on each sandwich, followed by one-fourth of the peppers and mushrooms. Top with ¼ cup Swiss cheese.

Put the sandwiches together, then press on a panini maker for 3 to 4 minutes. Serve each sandwich with ½ cup Au Jus, on the side.

SMOKEHOUSE MEATLOAF

Janet taught middle school English for several years and was very popular among the other teachers because of the lunches she brought to the teacher's lounge—especially on meatloaf day! Most people would not consider meatloaf haute cuisine, but smoke it with a mild wood such as pecan and it becomes what I like to call fine swine dining. We serve it in the restaurant every Wednesday with sides of Green Beans with Garlic (page 168) and boiled new potatoes sprinkled with feta cheese.

MAKES 2 LOAVES

- 2$^1/_2$ pounds lean ground beef
- 2$^1/_2$ pounds ground pork
- 1 medium celery rib, finely chopped
- 1 medium onion, finely chopped
- 1 clove garlic, finely minced
- 1 large egg, beaten
- $^1/_2$ cup breadcrumbs
- 2 tablespoons balsamic vinegar
- 1 tablespoon coarse sea salt
- $^1/_2$ tablespoon freshly ground black pepper
- $^1/_2$ cup The **Q** Company's Basic BBQ Sauce (page 42), plus extra for basting

In a large bowl, mix the ground beef and ground pork together by hand.

In a smaller bowl, combine the celery, onion, garlic, egg, breadcrumbs, vinegar, sea salt, pepper, and Basic BBQ Sauce.

Add the seasonings to the meat and mix by hand until just combined.

Bring the smoker up to between 225°F and 240°F.

Prepare two aluminum loaf pans with nonstick cooking spray. Shape the meat mixture into the loaf pans. Brush the top of each loaf with reserved Basic BBQ Sauce, and set the loaf pans in the smoker—or on the grill grate, away from the direct heat, if you're using a grill. Cover the smoker, then smoke the meatloaves for 2 to 3 hours, until the internal temperature reaches 190°F.

Remove the meatloaves from the smoker, then let them rest for at least 10 to 15 minutes. Serve immediately.

PATTY MELT

Great for leftover meatloaf.

SERVES 4

> 1 medium Vidalia onion, thinly sliced
> 1 green pepper, seeded and sliced
> 1 pint sliced mushrooms
> 4 slices Swiss cheese
> 8 slices Texas toast
> 4 thick slices Smokehouse Meatloaf (page 70)

Sauté sliced Vidalia onion, green pepper, and mushrooms in a skillet until they are caramelized, about 10 to 13 minutes.

Place a slice of Swiss cheese on each of two slices of Texas toast. Cut a thick slab of meatloaf and set it on one of the slices of bread, then smother it with the caramelized vegetables.

Place the other slice of bread on top, cheese side facing the meatloaf, then press in a panini maker for 90 seconds, until the bread is golden and crispy. Enjoy every bite.

> **Sipping Suggestion:** Fattier cuts of meat, like brisket and prime rib, stand up well to richly flavored beers like stouts, and full-bodied red wines, such as an inky Malbec from Argentina. Incorporating beer or wine into your barbecue sauce, or your braising or brining liquids will carry the grain and fruit undertones through the dish, complementing your beverage of choice.

SMOKEHOUSE MEATBALL AND PIMENTO CHEESE SANDWICH

A Southern twist on an Italian sub.

SERVES 4 TO 6

FOR THE MEATBALLS:

$1/2$ recipe Smokehouse Meatloaf (page 70), uncooked

1 cup The **Q** Company's Basic BBQ Sauce (page 42)

4 teaspoons orange blossom honey

FOR THE SANDWICHES:

8 to 12 slices Texas toast

2 cups Pimento Cheese (page 75)

Form the meatloaf mixture into approximately 18 to 24 (2-inch round) meatballs and place them in an aluminum pan with a cover. Freeze the meatballs overnight.

Bring the smoker up to 225°F and place the frozen meatballs in the pan on the smoker for at least 40 minutes, until the internal temperature reaches 150°F.

Remove the pan from the smoker and pour off any excess oil.

Mix the barbecue sauce with the honey and baste the meatballs with the mixture.

Place the pan of meatballs back into the smoker until the internal temperature reads 190°F, approximately 15 to 20 minutes. Brush with the honey-barbecue sauce once more before making the sandwiches.

(continued)

To assemble the sandwiches, butter 8 to 12 slices Texas toast on one side, then slather Pimento Cheese on the other sides. Arrange 4 meatballs on half of the slices, Pimento Cheese side up, then top with the other slices. The meatballs should be enveloped by the Pimento Cheese.

Press the sandwiches in a panini maker for 2 to 3 minutes. Serve immediately.

PIMENTO CHEESE

2 cups shredded cheddar cheese

1 (8-ounce) package cream cheese, softened

2 tablespoons finely grated onion

1 teaspoon granulated sugar

1/4 teaspoon celery salt

1/8 teaspoon freshly ground black pepper

1 (7-ounce) jar pimentos, drained and chopped

While the meatballs are smoking, prepare the Pimento Cheese by mixing together in a food processor the cheddar cheese, cream cheese, onion, sugar, celery salt, pepper, and pimentos. The Pimento Cheese should be smooth without apparent chunks of pimentos.

Store the pimento cheese in an airtight container in the refrigerator until you are ready to use. It can keep up to 1 week.

SPAGHETTI ON THE GRILL

Spaghetti can become one of those dishes that grows boring because you can get stuck in a rut making it the same tired way. Break the jar sauce mold and give this ol' standby a smoky makeover tonight.

SERVES 6

> 4 (15-ounce) cans tomato sauce
> 2 (15-ounce) cans diced tomatoes
> 3 cloves garlic, peeled and crushed
> 1 medium green bell pepper
> 1 small onion
> 2 tablespoons granulated sugar
> 1 tablespoon freshly ground black pepper
> 1 teaspoon dried basil
> 1 teaspoon The **Q** Company's Basic BBQ Sauce (page 42)
> 18 to 24 (1 serving) Smokehouse Meatballs (page 73)
> 1 pound spaghetti, cooked
> 1 cup freshly grated Parmesan cheese

Prepare the grill for medium heat.

Set a stockpot on the grill and add the tomato sauce, diced tomatoes, garlic, bell pepper, onion, sugar, black pepper, basil, and barbecue sauce. Stir together until well combined and let it come to a slow simmer for 20 minutes.

Add the cooked Smokehouse Meatballs to the sauce and simmer 10 to 15 minutes more, so the flavors can meld.

Serve a generous portion of sauce over $1/2$ to 1 cup cooked spaghetti per person. Sprinkle with freshly grated Parmesan cheese.

DEEP SOUTH ANTIPASTI PLATTER

Good food brings everybody to the table, and so does a party! This decidedly Southern take on the Italian antipasti platter is perfect for a Super Bowl party or as small bites before a big Thanksgiving meal. And you'll really impress your friends with how much you can elevate the flavors of typical school lunch fare.

SERVES 12

>   3- to 5-pound bologna chub
>   3- to 4-pound boneless country ham
>   1 whole Genoa salami in natural casing
>   10 Roma tomatoes
>   4 red peppers
>   Assortment of condiments

Peel off the wax or paper skin from the bologna and ham. Leave the salami in its natural casing.

Wash and pat the tomatoes and red peppers dry, and place them in an aluminum pan.

Using pecan wood for its subtlety and sweetness, bring the smoker up to between 220°F and 240°F, and place the meats and pan of tomatoes and peppers in the smoker. Cover the smoker and smoke until the meat reaches an internal temperature of 150°F. Smoke the tomatoes and peppers for approximately 2 hours. They will turn a concentrated dark reddish-brown around the edges.

Thinly slice the bologna, ham, and salami. Roll or fold the slices and fan them out on a serving tray.

(continued)

Once they are cool to the touch, peel the tomatoes and peppers. Remove the seeds from the peppers and slice the peppers into long strips. Place the strips on the serving tray. Put the tomatoes in a small bowl or spoon them onto the serving tray beside the peppers.

> Tip: You can also use the smoked tomatoes on bruschetta, dice them finely and mix them with a little olive oil, sea salt, and freshly ground black pepper, or incorporate them into your favorite salsa recipe.

Finish the platter with a variety of condiments for dipping and spreading, such as Pimento Cheese (page 75), The Q Company's Basic BBQ Sauce (page 42), Cajun Rémoulade (page 135), Black-Eyed Pea Hummus (page 181), and stone-ground mustard. Serve with sliced Sister Schubert's Parker House Style Rolls for sandwiches.

> Tip: Reserve the tomato and pepper oils that have collected in the bottom of the pan for use in homemade vinaigrette.

GRILLED RACK OF LAMB WITH ORANGE MARMALADE GLAZE

We wanted to include two of our favorite lamb recipes, both of which make impressive spreads for springtime celebrations such as Easter and Passover.

SERVES 4 TO 6

> 2 to 3 medium lamb racks, 7 to 8 bones per rack
> 1 cup Lamb Rub (page 39)
> Olive oil
> 1 cup Dijon mustard
> $^1/_2$ cup Grade A maple syrup
> 2 cups unseasoned breadcrumbs
> Orange Marmalade Glaze (page 82)

Wash the lamb racks under cool running water, then pat dry.

Massage the Lamb Rub into the flesh, then liquefy the spices with olive oil.

Mix the mustard and syrup together, then coat the racks with the mixture.

Press the breadcrumbs to form a crust on the outside of the racks, then put in the refrigerator for at least 3 hours to set and absorb the flavors.

Prepare the grill for indirect grilling over medium-high heat. Lay the lamb on one side, away from the direct heat, and grill for 4 to 6 minutes. Flip the racks to the other side and grill 4 to 6 minutes more. Remove one of the racks and test the temperature. Depending on the degree of doneness you desire, 130°F to 135°F is medium rare.

Remove the racks from the grill and let rest for 10 minutes before serving with a side of Orange Marmalade Glaze (page 82).

(continued)

ORANGE MARMALADE GLAZE

$1/2$ cup freshly squeezed orange juice
$1/2$ cup prepared orange marmalade
$1/4$ cup extra virgin olive oil
2 tablespoons freshly squeezed lemon juice
Pinch of fine sea salt
Pinch of white pepper
2 tablespoons butter

In a heavy-bottomed saucepan over medium heat, combine the orange juice, marmalade, oil, lemon juice, salt, and pepper. Stir and simmer for 15 minutes, until the marmalade has dissolved and the glaze has thickened slightly. Keep the sauce warm on low heat.

Stir in the butter to finish the glaze just before serving.

SMOKED LEG OF LAMB

SERVES 6 TO 8

> 1 (4- to 6-pound) leg of lamb
> 2 to 3 cups Lamb Marinade (page 33)
> 1 cup Lamb Rub (page 39)

Wash the leg of lamb under cold running water, then pat dry.

Place the leg and Lamb Marinade in a large plastic marinade bag. Close the bag and marinate overnight in the refrigerator.

Bring your smoker up to between 220°F and 240°F.

Remove the leg from the marinade, rinse the leg under cool running water, then pat dry.

Massage the rub liberally all over the leg, then place the leg in the smoker and cook until it reaches an internal temperature of 130°F to 135°F, which is rare.

Serve with roasted potatoes and a side of Orange Marmalade Glaze (page 82).

Sipping Suggestion: Lamb is a grassy, mildly gamey meat that pairs well with equally rich, earthy beers and wines. Stock a Sam Smith's Taddy Porter for the hopheads, and a Napa Valley Merlot with soft notes of blueberry and chocolate for the wine lovers.

PIG

I do not believe in tortured barbecue, where you kill it, grill it, send it through a buffalo chopper until it turns into a fine mesh, then store it in a five-gallon plastic container in your walk-in until you serve it, drowned in sauce and microwaved.

Pig is too precious for such insult. It is the Kobe beef of the American South, and must be treated with respect. You can go whole hog with pig, grilling thick, meaty bone-in chops, hickory-smoking fat slabs of belly, or mopping sauce on a rack of low-and-slow St. Louis–cut ribs. Pork basically can take anything—any seasoning, any spice, any wood, any amount of heat, and any kind of sauce—without losing itself. Makes me think of Wilbur in *Charlotte's Web*. "Some Pig," indeed.

One of our best competitions for ribs occurred in Louisville, Kentucky, at a KCBS competition. Our setup was right by the water, and it was so hot that day I didn't know if we would make it. But I still have that Louisville Slugger with "First Place in Ribs" on it, strategically placed on the wall in the shop near the cash register just in case it needs to do double duty. Our side competition for the mint julep didn't fare so well.

That was also the competition where we mentored another fellow, who was competing for the first time. He didn't have a tent or proper tools, and he was wilting beneath the heat—literally and figuratively. We helped him out, gave him some pointers, and he ended up joining the National Barbecue Association. In spite of the hardships, he fell hard for 'cue.

Like I said, barbecue is an addiction.

THE Q COMPANY'S PULLED PORK

This recipe was the one we used when we first started competing. And even though we were successful with it, it really made a mess—so be prepared to get slathered. This one creates a sweet-tangy crust, especially when smoked with woods such as hickory, cherry, or pecan. Finish it off with a vinegar-based sauce like Wiley's North Carolina Sauce (page 47) and you'll have the perfect balance of flavors—and the perfect bite. Although we use pork butt, this recipe is equally good for pork shoulder.

SERVES 6 TO 8

> 1 (5- to 6-pound) pork butt
> 1/4 cup freshly ground black pepper
> 1 cup firmly packed light brown sugar
> 1/4 cup The Q Company's Basic Rub (page 34)
> 1 jar prepared yellow mustard

Wash the pork butt under cold running water, then pat dry. Liberally coat the butt, first with the black pepper, then with the brown sugar, then with the Basic Rub. Liquefy the seasonings with the mustard.

Cover the pork butt with plastic wrap or aluminum foil and let it rest in the refrigerator for at least 6 hours, but preferably overnight.

Bring your smoker up to between 220°F and 240°F. Unwrap the pork butt and place it, fat side up, inside the smoker, or on the grill plate over a drip pan if you're using a grill. Cover the smoker and smoke the pork butt 6 to 8 hours, until the internal temperature reaches 190°F.

Remove the pork butt from the smoker and transfer it to a cutting surface. Tent the butt with aluminum foil and allow the meat to rest for at least 20 minutes.

(continued)

Wearing heavy-duty rubber or silicone gloves, pull the pork from the bone and shred, discarding any fat. You'll know you're a success when you can cleanly pull the bone straight out of the butt.

Serve the pulled pork immediately on a dinner plate or piled between two toasted hamburger buns with a side of barbecue sauce.

Tip: If you ever find yourself out of the Basic Rub, simply substitute a mixture of 1 cup seasoning salt and 1 cup freshly ground black pepper for a perfectly fine rub.

Sipping Suggestion: Pork is one of those meats where picking a beer or wine is completely dependent upon how the dish is prepared. The key: lead with the flavor profiles in the sauce, rub, marinade, and injection. Your wine choice should reflect the predominant flavors and aromas in your dish. (If you're not familiar with wine profiles, ask for guidance from a reputable wine shop.) For many of the recipes in this section, you can't go wrong with a dry rosé. If the dish is packing heat, pick a sweet wine, such as—dare we even suggest?!—white Zinfandel.

REDNECK NACHOS

If you ever find yourself with leftover pulled pork, make a platter of these for a late-night snack, a get-together with friends, or to serve at your next Super Bowl party.

SERVES 4 TO 6

> 1½ pounds potatoes, peeled
> Oil, for frying
> 10 ounces shredded sharp white cheddar cheese
> 1 cup heavy cream
> 14 ounces pulled pork shoulder or butt
> 1 (11-ounce) jar of sliced pickled jalapeño peppers
> ½ cup The Q Company's Basic BBQ Sauce (page 42)

Slice the potatoes into thin chips on a kitchen mandoline, so that the slices will be uniform and cook evenly. Pat the chips dry and set aside.

Pour enough oil in a deep fryer or heavy-bottomed Dutch oven to reach halfway up the sides. Heat the oil to at least 350° F. Meanwhile, combine the cheese and cream in a medium saucepan on medium heat, whisking occasionally until smooth and glossy. Turn heat to low to keep the sauce warm while the chips are frying.

Fry the chips in small batches until they are brown on the edges and crisped through. Drain the batches of chips on paper towels.

Spread the chips in baskets or on a platter lined with parchment paper. Sprinkle the pork across the chips, drizzle with cheese sauce, and strafe with jalapeño peppers and barbecue sauce to taste. Serve immediately.

> **Tip:** If you happen to be making Grown-up Mac 'n' Cheese (page 154), save a little of the cheese sauce from that recipe and use it for the cheese sauce in this one to add some herbaceous flavor layers.

SMOKEHOUSE CLUB

I surprised our cooks, as well as myself, with how good this particular variation on the traditional club turned out. To prove great minds think alike, I recently saw a photo of an almost identical sandwich on the cover of Taste of the South, *only it was spread with pimento cheese instead of mayo—a fine idea that we should try.*

SERVES 4

> 8 slices Texas toast
> 4 tablespoons mayonnaise
> 8 slices Fried Green Tomatoes (page 177)
> 8 lettuce leaves
> 12 strips thick-sliced smokehouse bacon
> 1 pound The Q Company's Pulled Pork (page 86)

Slather mayonnaise on each slice of Texas toast. Layer one Fried Green Tomato on each slice. On half the slices, place a lettuce leaf, 3 strips bacon, and 3 to 4 ounces pulled pork. Press the sandwich sides together, cut in half, then take a bite of heaven.

HEIRLOOM BACON

I live by the philosophy that good food ain't cheap and cheap food ain't good. Quality matters to me, and I look for the kinds of purveyors who share this ethic. One of those purveyors is Allan Benton of Benton's Smoky Mountain Country Hams in Madisonville, Tennessee. Benton has revived old-world methods of slowly dry curing ham over the course of nine to thirty months. He procures heirloom hogs raised on natural diets from small Midwestern and Southern farms. He is a rock star to highbrow chefs of four-star restaurants in New York City and Chicago. Last time I ordered, there was a four-week waiting list for his hams and hickory-smoked bacon.

ULTIMATE BLT

James Beard once said that "too few people understand a really good sandwich," and I couldn't agree more. The secret to a great BLT is the quality of the bacon. Don't just settle for that thin, fake-smoked stuff in the grocery store. I added this to our menu after tasting Allan Benton's salty-sweet slab of bacon. Sure, buying heirloom bacon is pricier, but it's worth it to me to get great taste, superior quality, and to help small, family-run businesses—kind of like mine—thrive in this country.

SERVES 6

1 pound thick-sliced smokehouse bacon
$^1/_2$ cup mayonnaise
$^1/_3$ cup stone-ground mustard
12 slices Texas toast
6 (1-ounce) slices Swiss cheese
1 cup shredded lettuce
1 medium tomato, thinly sliced

In a cast-iron skillet, cook the bacon over medium-high heat until it's brown and crisp. Drain and set aside.

While the bacon cooks, stir the mayonnaise and mustard together, then spread the "maystard" on each slice of bread. On half of the bread slices, alternate layers of cheese, lettuce, tomato, and bacon. Press the sandwich halves together, then cut in two. Serve immediately.

THE Q COMPANY'S RIBS

If I can teach one thing to my students—aside from internal temperature always prevails over time—it's to disabuse them of this notion that rib meat should be so tender it "falls off the bone." You'd be laughed off the competition circuit if you turned in a rib without meat on it. However, a rib should pull away cleanly from the bone as you eat it—holding it with your fingers, not cutting it away with a knife and fork.

SERVES 6 TO 8

> 2 to 3 racks pork ribs, St. Louis cut
> 1 cup The Q Company's Basic Rub (page 34)
> $^1/_4$ cup Garlic-Pepper Rub (page 37)
> Olive oil
> Wiley's Rib Spray (page 41)
> The Q Company's Basic BBQ Sauce (page 42)

Wash the ribs under cold water, then pat dry.

Set the ribs, meat side down, on a cutting surface. Use a butter knife or skewer to remove the silver skin on the underside of the ribs. The silver skin is the thick, shiny, opaque membrane that runs the length of the rack. Starting with the second bone, insert the knife or skewer between the membrane and the bone and remove the entire silver skin, holding onto it with a paper towel because it gets slippery. Make sure the entire silver skin is removed, because it will keep the rub from flavoring the meat and it is tough to chew. Repeat this procedure for each rack of ribs.

Coat the racks with the Basic Rub and massage the spices into the meat. (Rub is never the predominant flavor; it is only an accent.) You want to coat the ribs evenly, then sprinkle 2 or 3 pinches of the Garlic-Pepper Rub on both sides of the racks. Liquefy the rub with a generous dose of olive oil.

Store the ribs in a plastic bag in the refrigerator for at least 6 hours, but preferably overnight.

(continued)

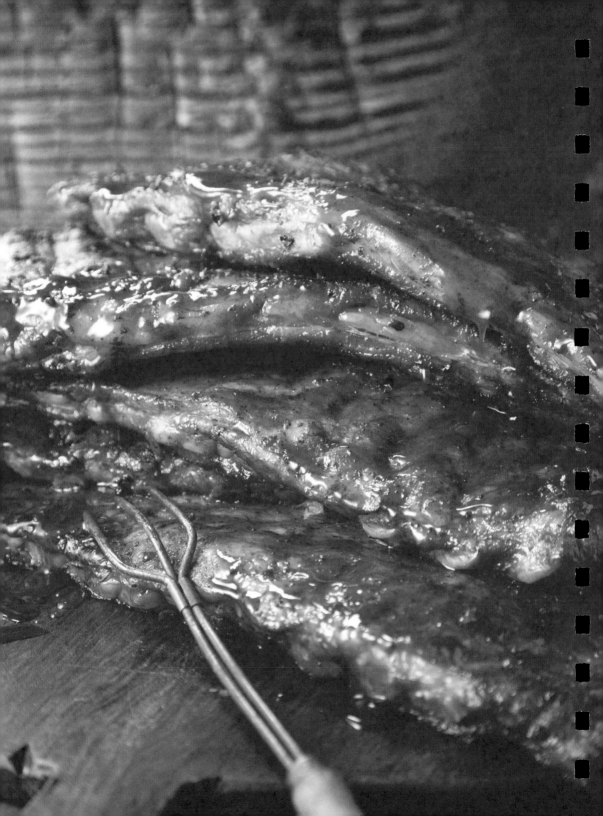

Bring the smoker up between 225°F and 240°F. Unwrap the ribs and place them meat side down on the grill grate. Leave the ribs in this position for the first hour, then flip the ribs and strafe them with the rib spray. After another hour, flip the ribs again and spray them to maintain their moisture.

When you're ready to flip the ribs, mop the underside with the barbecue sauce (the side that's up). Flip the ribs to meat side up, then mop the ribs again. Cook for another ½ hour, or until the ribs bend in the middle when picked up with tongs.

Remove the ribs from the grill, glaze them with sauce, then cover with foil and allow them to rest for 20 to 30 minutes before serving.

SMOKED BONE-IN PORK LOIN

Smoked pork loin has become a favorite of our regular customers, and we always run out when we have it on special. When it goes on sale at the Piggly Wiggly, I run down and buy them out so that we have plenty for shop and home. It goes great with a side of Collard Greens (page 170) and Wiley's Favorite BBQ Beans (page 161).

SERVES 8 TO 10

> 1 (8- to 10-pound) bone-in pork loin
> $\frac{1}{4}$ cup kosher salt
> $\frac{1}{4}$ cup coarsely ground black pepper
> $\frac{1}{4}$ cup The **Q** Company's Basic Rub (page 34)
> $\frac{1}{4}$ cup Lamb Rub (page 39)
> Olive oil

Wash the pork loin under cold running water, then pat dry.

Massage the salt, pepper, and rubs all over the pork loin, one at a time, then liquefy the seasonings with olive oil.

Wrap the loin in plastic wrap and let it rest at least 6 hours in the refrigerator, preferably overnight.

Bring the smoker up to 225°F. Unwrap the loin and set it in the smoker. Cover the smoker and cook until the internal temperature reaches 165°F.

Remove the loin from the smoker and let it rest for at least 10 to 15 minutes before serving.

CUBAN SANDWICH

A taste of the Caribbean.

SERVES 4

> 4 (6-inch) Cuban rolls
> Spicy brown mustard
> 8 Claussen Sandwich Slices pickles
> 8 slices Swiss cheese
> 8 slices black forest deli ham, or smoked country ham
> 1 pound sliced pork loin or pulled pork
> Unsalted butter, melted

To assemble the sandwiches, open up the Cuban rolls and slather each side with the mustard. Then place a pickle slice, Swiss cheese slice, ham slice, and 4 ounces pork loin on both sides of each roll.

Press the two halves of each roll together, then heat each roll in a sandwich press for approximately 5 minutes, until the cheese melts and the bread turns lightly golden.

Brush the top and bottom of the sandwich with melted butter, cut the sandwich in half, and serve.

BIRD

Janet calls chicken the little black dress of the culinary world. Because of its versatility, you can dress it up or down. Serve Smoked and Stuffed Chicken Breasts (page 107) for a special occasion, or Saturday Hot Wings (page 108) for a tailgate party.

For all its adaptability, chicken is, by far, the least forgiving of the four main meats—always a wild card. We used to have someone on The Q Company team designated as "the chicken man." He nursed the chickens after they came out of the smoker and made sure the skin didn't burn on the grill. Despite his best efforts, though, things could still turn from good to bad in a second—skin goes soggy, meat dries out. That's why we cherished the times when we placed in chicken—few though they were. It was a real team victory.

Sipping Suggestion: Just like "the other white meat," pairing wine and beer with poultry depends on the flavors predominant in the preparation. A creamy, rich Guinness balances well with the smokiness of barbecue. An un-oaked white Chardonnay with hints of tropical fruit goes great with the spicier dishes, while an oaked white Chardonnay complements the richness of turkey. Both *red* Zinfandel and a mild Shiraz (Syrah) from Australia offer wonderful alternatives. And Champagne and other sparkling wines bring out the best in crispy fried chicken and turkey.

THE Q COMPANY'S CHICKEN

The ultimate goal for prize-winning chicken: crispy skin and succulent flesh. For woods, use either straight pecan or a combination of pecan and cherry, with more of the former.

SERVES 4

> 1 ($3^{1}/_{2}$- to 4-pound) whole fresh chicken
> Basic Poultry Marinade (page 29) or The Q
>   Company's Chicken Marinade (page 30)
> Lemon-Pepper Rub (page 36)
> Olive oil
> The Q Company's Basic BBQ Sauce (page 42)

Remove the giblets and neck from the chicken. Rinse the chicken inside and out under cool running water. Pat dry.

On a clean cutting surface, use a sharp knife to trim the chicken of excess fat and skin. Cut the chicken in half.

Transfer the chicken to a marinating bag and pour in the marinade. Make sure all parts of the chicken are covered with the marinade, then place the bag in the refrigerator for at least 3 hours.

When you are ready to smoke the chicken, remove the chicken from the marinating bag, rinse the chicken inside and out, then pat dry.

With your index finger, loosen the skin on the chicken so that the flavor of the seasonings can permeate the chicken. Massage a generous amount of the Lemon-Pepper Rub onto and under the skin of the chicken. Liquefy the rub with olive oil, making sure to get under the skin.

Truss the chicken so that the more delicate parts of the chicken, such as the wings, are packed tightly against the bird.

(continued)

Bring the smoker up to between 220°F and 240°F. Smoke the chicken until the internal temperature reaches 165°F. Use a meat thermometer to check the internal temperature in several places. First, test the thickest part of the breast meat without touching the bone. Bones heat up faster and hotter and will give you a false reading. Then test the thigh. Go with the lowest temperature.

Once you pull the chicken from the smoker, cut it into quarters.

Optional step: If you want a sauced chicken, when the lowest temperature has reached 165°F, after approximately 1½ hours, transfer the chicken quarters to a barbecue sauce waller of your liking. To create the waller, pour the sauce in a deep aluminum foil pan. Submerge the chicken in the pan, covering almost the entire chicken with sauce. Tent the pan with aluminum foil so that the steam from the chicken can be released.

Once the chicken has steeped in the barbecue waller for at least 15 minutes, transfer the chicken back to the grill over indirect heat. If using coals, they should be ashy gray. Place the chicken skin side up first, and keep close watch; the sauce will burn easily because of its sugar content. Then flip the chicken to get good grill marks and some charring on the skin. Keep flipping until the internal temperature of the chicken reaches 180°F. Do not cover the grill.

Transfer the chicken to a platter, cover with foil, and allow the chicken to rest for at least 10 minutes before serving.

> Tip: Save the flavor-packed juices in the drip pan of the smoker to use in gravies, stews, or soups, or even a risotto.

SMOKED CHICKEN TWO WAYS

Smoked chicken is rather versatile and can be used any number of ways, from stuffing on potato skins to topping on flatbreads. Here are two of our favorite ways to use smoked chicken.

SMOKED FRIED CHICKEN

Hot and tasty.

SERVES 4

Follow the directions for smoking The Q Company's Chicken (page 102), but do not sauce the chicken.

Once the chicken has reached an internal temperature of 170°F, remove it from the smoker and cut the chicken into quarters. Deep-fry the quarters at 350°F in peanut or canola oil for 5 minutes. Remove the chicken from the oil and let drain. Serve hot and tasty with a side of gravy.

SMOKED CHICKEN SALAD

Cool and refreshing.

SERVES 4

> 1¹/₂ pounds smoked chicken meat, cooled and diced
> 6 hard-boiled eggs, finely chopped
> 4 celery ribs, finely chopped
> 1 cup mayonnaise
> 1 cup sweet pickle relish
> 1 tablespoon Better Than Bouillon Chicken Base
> 3 dashes hot sauce

In a large bowl, mix all of the ingredients together until well combined. Cover with plastic wrap and let sit in the refrigerator for 2 hours so that the flavors can meld. Serve as a sandwich, or scoop onto a salad.

SMOKED AND STUFFED CHICKEN BREASTS

When we cater weddings, brides often ask for something elegant and affordable. Smoked and Stuffed Chicken Breasts is my go-to dish to achieve that balance. Succulent and savory, it makes a colorful presentation and works well with almost any side. Serve it at your next fancy dinner party.

SERVES 4

> 4 (6- to 8-ounce) bone-in chicken breasts, skin on
> 1 red bell pepper, seeded and diced
> 1 green bell pepper, seeded and diced
> 1 large yellow onion, diced
> 1 pint baby bella mushrooms, diced
> 1 (4-ounce) jar of sun-dried tomatoes, diced
> 1 cup shredded Swiss cheese

Wash the chicken breasts under cool running water, then pat dry.

In a medium bowl, combine the red and green bell peppers, onion, mushrooms, and sun-dried tomatoes.

Use your finger to loosen the chicken skin and create a pocket, then stuff a quarter of the vegetable mixture beneath the skin of each breast.

Bring the smoker up to between 220°F and 240°F. Smoke until the internal temperature reaches 170°F. During the last 10 minutes of smoking, sprinkle ¼ cup cheese on each breast.

Remove the breasts from the grill and allow to rest for 10 minutes, then serve.

SATURDAY HOT WINGS

We adapted the traditional Buffalo wing recipe and serve our version on Saturdays at the shop. They are so good we had a family from New York come in and eat us right out of wings one night. Many of our regulars order them for parties, up to two hundred at a time. Trust me, they go fast. So if you want them, call ahead—or better yet, learn how to make them yourself.

SERVES 6 TO 8

> 10 pounds chicken wings
> 4 cups Frank's RedHot Original Cayenne Pepper Sauce
> Canola, vegetable, or peanut oil, for deep-frying

Rinse the chicken wings, then pat dry.

Place the chicken wings in a large bowl and pour the hot sauce all over them, until the wings are thoroughly immersed. Cover the bowl with plastic wrap and steep the wings overnight in the refrigerator.

Bring the smoker up to between 220°F and 240°F. Smoke the chicken wings until the internal temperature reaches 165°F.

In a large stockpot or deep fryer, bring the oil to 350°F. Fry the chicken wings in small batches for 5 minutes each, until the skin is crispy and golden.

Serve the wings hot with a side of ranch or blue cheese dressing and celery sticks.

SMOKED CORNISH GAME HENS

Cornish game hens are little sponges for whatever flavoring they soak in. The bright, tart Mojo Sauce (page 32) enhances their juiciness with the flavor of the islands. Black Beans and Yellow Rice (page 167) provides the perfect accompaniment.

SERVES 4

> **4 Cornish game hens**
> **3 cups Mojo Sauce (page 32)**

Wash the hens under cool running water and pat dry.

Place the hens and Mojo Sauce in zip-lock plastic bags and marinate up to 12 hours in the refrigerator.

When you are ready to smoke the hens, set them in an aluminum pan and let them come to room temperature, approximately 15 minutes.

Bring the smoker up to between 220°F and 240°F. Smoke the hens until their internal temperature reaches 170°F.

Allow the hens to rest 10 minutes before serving, along with the pan juices.

SMOKED TURKEY

If you really want to impress your friends and family at the holidays, smoke a turkey for dinner. It's simple, gives the smoker in the family something to do for several hours, and leaves your oven free to make Sweet Potato Casserole (page 158). Smoking works best for moderate-sized birds. If you need to feed more people than a 12-pounder can accommodate, smoke two birds.

SERVES 6 TO 10

> 1 (10- to 12-pound) whole fresh turkey, giblets removed
> 1 cup Cajun Rub (page 38)
> ¼ cup olive oil
> 4 cups water (optional)

Remove the neck and giblets package from inside the turkey. Rinse the bird inside and out, then pat dry.

Truss the bird by pinning the wings to the body with toothpicks, then do the same with the loose skin around the neck. Because these areas are thin, they tend to cook faster and may burn, so you may want to cover these tender areas with foil during the smoking process.

Massage the Cajun Rub into the skin of the bird, then loosen the skin around the breast and rub the spice blend directly on the meat. Follow the same process with the olive oil, then set the bird aside at room temperature while you prepare the smoker, approximately 30 minutes.

Rub a small amount of olive oil on the smoker or grill grate, depending on your smoker of choice, to keep the turkey from sticking. Bring the smoker up to between 225°F and 240°F. If you are smoking the bird on a grill, place an aluminum pan, holding approximately 4 cups water, in the middle of the coals. This water pan will catch the drippings for the turkey gravy, and the water will evaporate over the cooking time, helping to keep the bird moist.

Place the turkey in the center of the cooking grate directly over the water-drip pan and cover. Smoke the turkey for approximately 30 minutes per pound; therefore a 10-pound bird will cook for at least 5 hours. Try not to open the smoker and check on the bird too often, as the heat needs to remain constant for the bird to cook properly.

When you think the bird might be done, use a meat thermometer to check the internal temperature in several places. First, test the thickest part of the breast meat without touching the bone. Bones heat up faster and hotter and will give you a false reading. Then test the thigh. Go with the lowest temperature. When the lowest temperature reaches between 170°F and 180°F, transfer the turkey to a platter and cover tightly with aluminum foil.

Let the bird rest for at least 15 minutes so the juices can reconstitute and the bird stays warm for serving.

> **Tip:** You may substitute the Garlic-Pepper or Lemon-Pepper rubs, or simply season with coarse sea salt and coarsely ground black pepper. Also, feel free to experiment with fresh rosemary and sage. Our pit master, Marion, often fills the bird's cavity with halved lemons, onions, and fresh, fragrant herbs to infuse the turkey and the gravy made from the drippings with subtle flavors. Be sure to discard the "stuffing" before you serve the bird.

(continued)

The Day of Great Thanksgiving

We live in one of the most charitable-minded towns in America, and Janet and I have made giving back a part of our business culture. I highly recommend any business to build philanthropy into its budget and to stick to it.

For several years, I volunteered to cook the turkeys for the Old Savannah City Mission's Day of Great Thanksgiving, an outreach effort to feed the homeless and struggling families during the holidays. To the sounds of a gospel choir, we fed 1,300 people down the center sidewalk of Forsyth Park the first year. It was one of those experiences where the barriers between people fell away as volunteers and those in need broke bread together. We worked over two full days and nights with volunteers to season a hundred 10- to 12-pound turkeys, supplied by one of my vendors, and smoked them in two mobile pits.

The next year we worked over three days, smoked more than 300 turkeys, and fed 3,500 people. Each subsequent year the numbers swelled. The following year we brought in a third pit and smoked 500 turkeys. More than 1,000 volunteers helped serve more than 5,200 people, many of them families hit hard by the economic downturn. The next year, more than 6,000 people came to the park for Thanksgiving dinner.

That's a lot of birds, but it shows what you can do when you put your heart and skills behind something. I can't sing. I can't dance, and I can't act. But I sure can cook.

DEEP-FRIED TURKEY

Before you even think about deep-frying a turkey, you must follow these safety measures:

- *Wear protective clothing: long pants or jeans, closed-toe leather shoes, a long-sleeved shirt, and garden or leather work gloves. I don't care how warm the weather might be, never—ever—wear shorts or flip-flops. That might be silly advice to someone up North, but it's necessary to remind people who live in the South and along the coast.*

- *Always keep a working fire extinguisher nearby.*

- *Do not attempt to fry a frozen turkey or one that is even partially thawed. A fresh turkey works best.*

- *Do not put out a grease fire with water. Oil and water don't mix, and water will cause the fire to spread rather than squelch it. Instead, use sand, baking soda, or flour to suffocate the flames. In fact, keep a supply close at hand just in case.*

- *Never attempt to cook the mother of all turkeys. A 10- to 12-pound turkey works best for frying. Anything beyond that size creates a safety hazard because you will have difficulty lifting the bird out of the fryer. (And it will not come out as crispy as it should.)*

- *Keep children and pets away from the cooking area.*

- *The best place to fry a turkey is in the middle of an open space. Never fry a turkey on a wooden deck or inside a garage or carport.*

- *Never leave the hot oil or the frying turkey unattended—not even for a minute!*

- *As with any grilling or smoking, delay your alcohol consumption until after your turkey frying is complete. If you are worried that your friends or family will get ahead of you, get a funnel so you can catch up when you're finished.*

- *Always use the turkey stand and retriever hanger that came with your turkey frying kit.*

SERVES 10 TO 15

    1 (10- to 12-pound) turkey
    1 cup Cajun Rub (page 38)
    Cooking oil, preferably peanut or canola

Remove the packet of giblets. Wash the turkey under cool running water inside and out, then pat dry.

Generously massage Cajun Rub all over the turkey, underneath the skin, and inside the cavity.

Pour the oil into your fryer (follow the instructions that came with your turkey deep-fryer as to how much oil to use) and heat it to between 350°F and 375°F; this takes approximately 30 minutes.* Use a long-stemmed thermometer to keep track of the oil temperature.

When your oil reaches the desired temperature, slowly lower the turkey into the fryer, making sure not to tip over the fryer or let the oil splatter. The oil temperature will drop at first, but will soon return to the desired range. The flash point for oil, or the lowest temperature for it to ignite, is 412°F, so it is important to maintain the temperature between 350°F and 375°F.

The turkey is finished frying when its skin is crisp and the internal temperature of the thickest part of the meat not next to a bone measures 175°F on an instant-read thermometer. (You will need to lift the turkey out of the fryer to measure the temperature.) Reaching this temperature will take approximately 30 minutes to 1 hour, depending upon the size of the bird.

Let the turkey rest for at least 15 minutes before slicing it so that the juices can reconstitute.

---

* Technology has given us the oil-less infrared fryer, which saves on time, calories, and safety, and works just as well as a traditional turkey fryer. I've used one for the past few Thanksgivings, except last year, when I discovered well into the cooking process that it had broken. We had to resort to the old standby oven.

FISH AND CRUSTACEANS

The myth goes something like this: the closer you get to the coast, the worse the barbecue. I think whoever spread such slander is rather short-sighted; he's obviously never enjoyed a smoked oyster slow roasted over pecan wood or Citrus Shrimp (page 126) fresh off the grill.

Savannah, being a port city, enjoys an abundance of blue crab, Wild Georgia Shrimp, flounder, and other seafood. When Florida lobster season begins, we stock up on that sweet, succulent tail. Even if you are landlocked, there's plenty of other seafood that stands up well to grilling: salmon, halibut, cod, ahi tuna, swordfish, mahimahi, sea bass, tilapia, and crab (in the form of crab cakes). Just make sure when you are selecting fish to grill that you choose fillets cut from the thickest part of the fish. And get a grill

basket—it's a wise investment.

Because Janet and I eat lunch in the restaurant several times a week, we grill seafood most nights when we cook at home. When Janet organized three three-ring binders of recipes I had stuffed in various notebooks, she discovered I'd collected far more seafood recipes than any other kind. (But I pale in comparison to our next-door neighbor Bill, who has about five thousand shrimp recipes. No lie!)

I return time and again to BBQ Salmon (page 119) and Black Iron Skillet Cod with Garlic Butter (page 124), both of which always produce a flavor-filled, flakey fish. They are quick, easy dishes that fit well into busy life-styles. But we also take time to indulge in richer fare, like the Seafood Casserole (page 138) we served at our wedding.

PACIFIC SALMON

The rich taste and deep orange red color of wild-caught salmon shames the bland farm-raised varieties with their fake tans, which may also be filled with antibiotics and other chemicals. Anything labeled Atlantic salmon typically denotes fish that has been farm raised. But there are all kinds of wild salmon that are freshest at different times of the year.

Several years ago, I found a *Seattle Post-Intelligencer* article that helped clear up any confusion I'd had about salmon and when they run. Market prices for wild salmon vary wildly, yet this handy little outline should help you shop in season to get the best flavor and the best prices.

The **chinook,** also aptly known as the **king,** makes its run during the springtime. It often weighs more than thirty pounds. Its sunset-colored flesh is oily and intense.

The **sockeye,** with its bright red hue, weighs between six and ten pounds. With less oil, it is milder in flavor.

The pinkish orange **coho,** weighing in at ten to twenty pounds, is the salmon most likely to end up smoked or pickled.

The wee **pinks** are the favored choice of canneries, and are used most often for croquettes and cakes.

BBQ SALMON WITH SHALLOT-DILL SAUCE

When I was competing, I ran a contest-within-the-contest called "Anything Butt, Anything Goes." The purpose: to showcase regional specialties. A great competitive cook took top prize in the Pacific Northwest with this recipe, which had been in her family for more than fifty years and which she happily shared with me. Damon Lee Fowler—a cookbook author and apostle of historic Savannah cuisine—wrote an article for the Savannah Morning News *about our restaurant right after we opened in 2008. In it, he included this recipe. Since then, numerous people have come to the restaurant to tell us how often they've served this recipe and shared it with others.*

SERVES 4

> $^1/_2$ cup vegetable oil
> $^1/_4$ cup soy sauce
> Juice of $^1/_2$ lemon
> 2–3 drops hot sauce
> 1 clove garlic, minced
> 1 tablespoon finely chopped fresh dill
> 4 (8- to 10-ounce) skin-on salmon fillets, preferably wild caught such as coho or sockeye
> Shallot-Dill Sauce (page 121)

In a gallon-sized plastic bag with a double-seal enclosure, mix together the oil, soy sauce, lemon juice, hot sauce, garlic, and dill until well combined. Seal and set aside.

Rinse the fish under cold running water and pat dry.

Place the fish in the bag, seal, and allow to marinate in the refrigerator for no more than 30 minutes. (Never marinate seafood for very long, because the acid from the citrus will "cook" it.)

(continued)

While the fish marinates, prepare the grill for indirect cooking on low heat, bringing the grill to between 225°F and 240°F.

When the grill is ready, remove the salmon from the plastic bag and place in an aluminum pan or on foil in the middle of the grill. Reserve the remaining marinade for basting.

Cover the grill and cook the fish for 25 minutes, basting every 10 minutes. The fish is done when it easily flakes with a fork. Serve immediately with a side of Shallot-Dill Sauce.

> **Sipping Suggestion:** An amber or Scotch ale is the beer of choice for barbecued salmon, but if you just smoke it without the marinade, opt for a hefeweizen or hoppy IPA. A juicy Pinot Noir will offset some of the sweetness in the barbecue, as would a dry rosé. For a simplified version, serve a crisp, clean Sauvignon Blanc from California or New Zealand.

SHALLOT-DILL SAUCE

Cool and creamy.

MAKES 2¹/₄ CUPS

2 cups mayonnaise
2 whole shallots, peeled and finely chopped
3 tablespoons finely chopped fresh dill
1¹/₄ teaspoons apple cider vinegar
Juice and zest of 2 lemons
¹/₂ teaspoon fine sea salt
¹/₄ teaspoon freshly ground black pepper

In a medium bowl, mix all of the ingredients until well combined.

Serve with smoked, poached, or grilled salmon.

SMOKED SALMON AND CORN SALAD

A refreshing summer delicacy.

FOR THE DRESSING:

$^3/_4$ cup extra virgin olive oil

$^1/_4$ cup balsamic vinegar

4 shallots, minced

2 cloves garlic, minced

6 tablespoons chopped fresh basil

3 tablespoons finely chopped fresh parsley

Fine sea salt

Freshly ground black pepper

FOR THE SALAD:

6 cups fresh or frozen Silver Queen corn kernels, cooked

1 cup flaked smoked salmon

1 cup cherry tomatoes, quartered

$^1/_2$ red bell pepper, diced

3 tablespoons minced green onion

In a medium bowl, mix together the oil, vinegar, shallots, garlic, basil, and parsley. Adjust to taste with salt and pepper.

Set aside for at least 1 hour to allow the flavors to come together.

In a large bowl, toss together the corn, salmon, tomatoes, pepper, and green onion.

Drape with the dressing, then toss again until all ingredients are covered. Taste and adjust seasonings as necessary.

BLACK IRON SKILLET COD WITH GARLIC BUTTER

This dish is one of my all-time favorites. You can substitute another firm-fleshed fish, such as halibut, if cod is not readily available. And even if the garlic looks burned, those little crunchy bits taste great. Garnish the fish with sun-dried tomatoes in oil or just a squeeze of lemon juice.

SERVES 4

> 4 (1-inch thick) cod fillets
> 2 tablespoons olive oil
> 1 tablespoon Old Bay Seasoning
> 8 tablespoons (1 stick) unsalted butter
> 3 tablespoons minced garlic in oil
> 2 tablespoons freshly squeezed lemon juice

Rinse the cod fillets beneath cold running water, then pat dry.

Rub both sides of the cod fillets with the olive oil, then lightly sprinkle Old Bay Seasoning over the fish and rub it in.

In a cast-iron skillet, melt the butter over medium heat with the garlic and lemon juice. Add the cod fillets and cook for 6 minutes. Flip the fillets and cook a few minutes more, until the fish flakes easily and has reached 130°F. Serve immediately.

> **Sipping Suggestion:** A light lager is the perfect complement to the cod. In wines, you need something that can stand up to the garlic butter, such as a Viognier or Pinot Gris. For reds, go with a Rioja from Spain or a Nebbiolo from Italy.

GRiLLiNG FiSH

It's surprising how simple yet so intensely flavored grilled fish can be, all at the same time. Just about any firm-fleshed fish that can be cut into steaks or at least 1-inch-thick fillets is suitable for grilling. That list includes salmon, halibut, cod, ahi tuna, swordfish, mahimahi, monkfish, snapper, and trout, among others.

When grilling fish there are a few things to remember:

- Fish needs liquid to keep it from drying out on the grill. Marinate your fish for at least 15 minutes, but not more than ½ hour, to keep it moist while it's standing up to high heat.

- Invest in a wire mesh grill basket. Not only will it prevent the fish from sticking to the grill, which should be brushed with olive or vegetable oil, it will also produce distinctive cross-hatch marks for added texture.

- Experiment with pouches and planks as different methods of grilling fish for added flavor. Use skewers for fun and festive presentations.

Tip: For a list of fish good for both consumers and the earth, consult the Monterey Bay Aquarium's Seafood Watch program, www.montereybayaquarium.org/cr/seafoodwatch.aspx.

CITRUS SHRIMP

Because we live on the coast, we are blessed with easy access to fresh seafood. During the summer, Wild Georgia Shrimp tastes sweetest, and during those sweltering months, shrimp or a locally caught fish is on our table for dinner most nights. Any time you are grilling shrimp, you must use large shrimp. Jumbo or colossal work even better. This brightly flavored dish makes a perfect summer meal when served on a bed of coleslaw with a crisp-as-a-pear glass of chilled Pinot Gris to wash it down. Sweet tea is just fine too.

SERVES 4

> 24 fresh shrimp, 31/35 or larger
> Zest and juice of 1 medium orange
> Zest and juice of 1 fresh lime
> 1/4 cup dark rum
> 1/4 cup vegetable oil
> 4 cloves garlic, minced
> 2 teaspoons finely chopped fresh oregano
> 1 teaspoon granulated sugar
> 1/4 teaspoon sea salt
> 1/8 teaspoon coarsely ground black pepper

Soak 4 bamboo skewers in cold water for at least 30 minutes.

Peel and devein the shrimp, leaving the tails on. Set aside in the refrigerator until the marinade is ready.

For the marinade, in a large bowl, whisk together the juice and zest of the orange and lime, rum, oil, garlic, oregano, sugar, salt, and pepper until well combined.

Toss the shrimp in the marinade, cover with plastic wrap, and chill in the refrigerator for at least 30 minutes.

(continued)

Meanwhile, prepare the grill for direct grilling on medium heat, between 325°F and 375°F. Set the grill approximately 3 to 4 inches above the heat source.

Place 6 shrimp on each skewer, piercing them just above the tail and through the thickest part of the head. Reserve remaining marinade for basting.

Once the grill has reached the desired heat, place the skewers on the grill. Baste the shrimp with the marinade, then turn each skewer after 3 minutes. Remove the shrimp from the grill once they have turned a pinkish color all over and their tails have curled. Their total cooking time is between 5 and 7 minutes. Serve immediately.

A SHORT STUDY ON SHRIMP

WHAT TO LOOK FOR: Seek out purveyors of shrimp harvested in U.S. waters, such as the Gulf of Mexico or the southeastern Atlantic. The Gulf shrimp season typically runs from July through May, and the Atlantic shrimp season from April through January, depending upon temperatures and shrimp samples. If samples are running small, then the National Marine Fisheries Service can call for a shortened season to allow the shrimp population to rebound.

Americans consume more than four pounds of shrimp per person per year. Almost 80 percent of all shrimp is imported into the States from places such as Thailand where shrimp farmers exist beyond the purview of U.S. environmental standards. They cheaply cultivate the shrimp in ponds, feeding them an artificial diet of grains.

Wild Georgia Shrimp, on the other hand, must meet rigorous quality control standards established by the Georgia Shrimp Association. Shrimp trawlers must use nets equipped with devices that allow sea turtles and other marine life to escape to maintain the ocean's biodiversity. Because the shrimp feed on a natural diet, they are higher in protein and other heart-healthy vitamins and minerals, and lower in

fats and carbohydrates. Same is true for Gulf shrimp.

GO WITH YOUR NOSE: Give fresh shrimp the sniff test. It should smell like the ocean—briny and organic, and not at all fishy. Purchase fresh (and frozen) shrimp with their shells on to maintain moisture and flavor. Cook fresh shrimp within twenty-four hours of purchase.

COUNT MATTERS: Go by count, not size, when purchasing shrimp, because the amount of shrimp per pound determines the best type of cooking method (e.g., colossal are great for grilling; large and jumbo for Lowcountry boils) as well as the number of servings per person. One pound of uncooked shrimp with the shells on will yield a half pound cooked and peeled. Only use shrimp classified as large or bigger for grilling.

Extra Colossal	Under 10 shrimp/pound (U/10)
Super Colossal	Under 12/pound (U/12)
Colossal	Under 15/pound (U/15)
Extra Jumbo	16–20/pound (16/20)
Jumbo	21–25/pound (21/25)
Extra Large	26–30/pound (26/30)
Large	31–35/pound (31/35)
Medium Large	36–40/pound (36/40)
Medium	41–50/pound (41/50)
Small	51–60/pound (51/60)
Extra Small	61–70/pound (61/70)

JANET'S SHRIMP 'N' GRITS

During a side contest for grits on the grounds of the Georgia BBQ Championship in Dillard, Janet won two years in a row with this recipe using yellow Carolina Plantation Stone Ground Grits, which are 100 percent natural. Although shrimp 'n' grits have assumed delicacy status on many dinner menus across the country, it remains a hearty workingperson's breakfast around these parts. It was a staple of the Gullah/Geechee culture on the barrier islands between North Carolina and Florida, as well as for fishermen and shrimpers heading out in the darkness for the day's catch.

SERVES 6

3 cups prepared grits, preferably yellow Carolina
    Plantation Stone Ground Grits

4 tablespoons unsalted butter, divided

1 pound julienned country ham

1 pound sliced smoked pork sausage

$1^1/_2$ pounds fresh shrimp, peeled, deveined, rinsed, and drained

1 pound bay scallops, rinsed and patted dry (optional)

8 cloves fresh garlic, minced

Pinch of Cajun spice

1 cup diced scallions

1 cup diced fresh tomatoes

4 tablespoons water

Prepare the grits according to package directions and keep warm.

In a large skillet, melt 1 tablespoon butter over medium-high heat and sauté the ham and sausage until slightly browned. Add the shrimp and scallops and sauté for 1 to 2 minutes more.

Add the garlic and Cajun spice, coating the shrimp and scallops, and sauté for approximately 30 seconds more.

Add the scallions, tomatoes, water, and remaining butter, and cook for approximately 30 seconds more, deglazing the skillet by scraping up the tasty brown bits on the bottom.

Spoon $\frac{1}{2}$ cup grits onto each plate, then top with the shrimp mixture in equal portions. Serve immediately.

SHRIMP SALAD

Any Savannahian worth his or her salt has a shrimp salad recipe in their repertoire. Just like chicken, it can be dressed up or down. On casual days, serve it on a toasted Cuban roll or with crackers. Fancy it up for a special occasion as a scoop in a hollowed-out tomato. Sneak in some chopped hard-boiled egg for richer texture and flavor.

SERVES 6 TO 8

> 1 pound fresh large shrimp, cooked, peeled, and deveined
> 1 celery stalk with leaves, coarsely chopped
> 1 medium shallot, coarsely chopped
> 1 cup mayonnaise
> Juice of 1 lemon
> 2 teaspoons Spanish paprika
> 1 teaspoon lemon zest
> 1 teaspoon Old Bay Seasoning
> 1 teaspoon freshly ground black pepper
> 2 drops hot sauce

Whether you grill, boil, or sauté the shrimp, allow it to cool, then coarsely chop it.

Gently fold the shrimp and remaining ingredients together in a large bowl to create a creamy, yet chunky, salad.

Cover the bowl with plastic wrap and chill in the refrigerator for at least 2 hours to allow the flavors to meld.

JANET'S CRAB CAKES WITH CAJUN RÉMOULADE

Whether you're catering a wedding or throwing a small get-together, crab cakes is one of the best dishes for entertaining. Janet started making these small cakes just after we got married, and we've served them as appetizers at nearly every party. The great thing: you can make these ahead and freeze them, uncooked. All you have to do is grill or sauté them just before serving.

SERVES 12

2 large eggs, whites only
2 cups mayonnaise, divided
6 tablespoons finely ground cracker crumbs, preferably Ritz
$3/4$ teaspoon dry mustard
$1/2$ teaspoon Old Bay Seasoning
$1/2$ teaspoon ground celery seed
$1/2$ teaspoon cayenne pepper
Juice of 2 lemons
1 pound lump crabmeat
8 slices dried white bread, or 2 cups panko breadcrumbs
4 tablespoons butter
Cajun Rémoulade (page 135)

In a large bowl, combine the egg whites and 1 cup mayonnaise; whisk until well combined. Whisk in the cracker crumbs, mustard, Old Bay, celery seed, cayenne pepper, and lemon juice until there are no lumps.

Gently fold in the crabmeat. Add more mayonnaise as necessary to get the desired consistency—clingy but not soupy.

Cover the bowl with plastic wrap and chill the mixture in the refrigerator for at least 1 hour.

(continued)

Meanwhile, cut and discard the crusts from the white bread (or freeze them for future use in turkey stuffing). Cut the bread into quarters, then pulse in a food processor fitted with a steel blade until you get a uniform small crumb. Place the breadcrumbs in a shallow dish.

Place a wire rack over a sheet pan. Remove the crab mixture from the refrigerator. Using a tablespoon, shape the chilled crab mixture into 2-inch cakes.

Dredge each cake in the breadcrumbs and set them on the wire rack. Chill the crab cakes for at least 30 minutes to allow the breading to set.

In a cast-iron skillet, melt the butter over medium-high heat. Sauté the crab cakes for 2 to 3 minutes per side, until golden brown and cooked through.

Drain the cakes on paper towels, then serve hot with a side of Cajun Rémoulade.

Sipping Suggestion: Crab, lobster, and shrimp are the rich succulents of the sea, and open the palate up to a great variety of beer and wine. For creamy dishes, buttery Chardonnays, yeasty sparkling wines, Marsannes, Roussannes, and Viogniers are all possible pairings. Pilsners and stouts hold their own.

CAJUN RÉMOULADE

Hot and spicy.

MAKES 2¹/₂ CUPS

    1 cup mayonnaise or plain Greek yogurt
    ¹/₂ cup chopped celery
    ¹/₂ cup chopped green onions
    2 tablespoons chopped fresh parsley
    2 tablespoons capers
    2 tablespoons prepared horseradish sauce
    1 tablespoon Dijon mustard
    1 tablespoon ketchup
    1 tablespoon Worcestershire sauce
    1 tablespoon apple cider vinegar
    1 tablespoon freshly squeezed lemon juice
    1 tablespoon hot sauce
    1 tablespoon paprika
    ¹/₂ teaspoon kosher salt

In a food processor fitted with a steel blade, place the mayonnaise or yogurt, celery, onions, and parsley. Pulse until the mixture is blended and the greens are coarsely minced. Add the remaining ingredients and pulse 3 or 4 times, until well combined, stopping in between to scrape down the sides.

You can serve this versatile sauce with crab, oysters, shrimp, or smoked bologna.

CRAB-STUFFED MUSHROOMS

A lot of catering calls for one-bites—robust finger foods that you can pop in your mouth without fumbling with a fork and spilling your cocktail. The perfect edible container, of course, is the mushroom cap, and you can fill it with just about anything savory.

SERVES 6 TO 8

>   1 tablespoon unsalted butter
>   1 medium Vidalia onion, finely diced
> $1/2$ pound smoked chicken or pulled pork, finely diced
> $1/2$ pound lump crabmeat, finely diced
>   3 ounces cream cheese, softened
> $1/4$ cup mayonnaise
> $1/4$ cup grated Parmesan cheese
> $1/4$ teaspoon freshly ground black pepper
>   2 drops hot sauce
>   1 pound fresh button mushrooms, cleaned, stems removed

Position a rack in the middle of the oven and preheat the oven to 350°F. Spray a sheet pan with nonstick cooking spray and set aside.

Melt the butter in a skillet over medium heat. Add the onion and sweat until tender and translucent, approximately 5 to 7 minutes. Drain the onion on layers of paper towels and set aside to cool.

In a large bowl, combine all the remaining ingredients except the mushrooms. Add the cooled onion and stir until thoroughly combined.

Arrange the mushroom caps on the sheet pan, then spoon the crab mixture into the caps. Bake the caps in the oven for 45 minutes to 1 hour, until the caps have tanned and the stuffing has turned golden. Serve immediately.

Tip: Freeze the mushroom stems to make vegetable stock with later.

GRILLED LOBSTER WITH CRAB IN CREAM

At an "Anything Butt, Anything Goes" competition in Mobile, Alabama, Buddy Babb of Paradise Ridge Catering made this prize-winning succulent and decadent dish. I asked him if I could purloin it to add to my catering menu.

SERVES 6 TO 8

> 8 (5-ounce) Florida rock lobster tails, in the shell
> 8 tablespoons (1 stick) butter
> 2 (4-ounce) cans mushrooms, coarsely chopped
> 2 cloves garlic, peeled and crushed
> $1/2$ cup each chopped fresh parsley and spinach
> $2/3$ cup all-purpose flour
> 2 cups light cream
> 1 (10.34-ounce) can chicken broth
> $1/2$ pound lump crabmeat

Prepare the grill for direct grilling on medium heat, between 325°F and 375°F. Grill the lobster tails for 3 minutes per side, then plunge them in a bath of ice water to stop cooking. Set aside.

In a cast-iron skillet set over the grill, melt the butter, then sauté the mushrooms until they have darkened, approximately 3 minutes. Add the parsley and spinach and sauté until they are bright green but wilted.

Sprinkle the flour in the pan and stir until it has dissolved. Stir in the cream and chicken broth. Continue to stir until the sauce starts to thicken.

Pull the cooled lobster meat from the shells, making sure to remove the membrane. Coarsely chop the lobster and crabmeat and add to the cream mixture. When thickened to the desired consistency, spoon it into the shells and serve.

SEAFOOD CASSEROLE

While my signature dish at our wedding was the Smoked Beef Tenderloin with Roquefort Sauce (page 63), Janet chose this salt water–inspired casserole (based on a recipe from our friend Sandra) as a nod to her Massachusetts upbringing. It, too, is given a place of honor on our sideboard during celebrations, taking on special significance because we are able to showcase Georgia's fresh coastal bounty. Start the recipe early in the day, as it needs to rest in the refrigerator for eight hours.

SERVES 8

- 1 cup dry white wine
- 4 tablespoons butter, divided
- 1 tablespoon chopped fresh parsley
- 1 teaspoon fine sea salt
- 1 medium onion, thinly sliced
- 1 pound fresh medium-sized shrimp (41/50), peeled and deveined
- 1 pound fresh bay scallops
- 3 tablespoons all-purpose flour
- 1 cup half-and-half
- $1/2$ cup grated Swiss cheese
- 2 teaspoons fresh lemon juice
- $1/8$ teaspoon pepper
- $1/2$ pound fresh lump crabmeat
- 1 (4-ounce) can sliced mushrooms
- 1 cup soft breadcrumbs
- $1/3$ cup freshly grated Parmesan cheese
- Paprika

Lightly butter a 7-by-11-inch baking dish and set aside. Combine the wine, 1 tablespoon butter, parsley, salt, and onion in a Dutch oven, and bring to a boil over medium heat.

Add the shrimp and scallops, cooking 3 to 5 minutes, until the shrimp curl and turn pink.

Remove the shrimp and scallops from the heat and drain, reserving $^2/_3$ cup of the liquid for later.

Melt the remaining 3 tablespoons butter in the Dutch oven over low heat. Add the flour and stir constantly to create a roux.

Gradually add the half-and-half, and cook over medium heat, stirring constantly until the mixture is thick and bubbly. Stir in the Swiss cheese. Gradually stir in the reserved liquid, lemon juice, and pepper until well combined. Add the shrimp mixture, crab, and mushrooms.

Spoon the mixture into the prepared baking dish and let cool. Cover with foil and refrigerate for 8 hours, allowing the flavors to meld.

Remove the baking dish from the refrigerator and let it come to room temperature. Preheat the oven to 350°F, then bake the casserole for 40 minutes.

Meanwhile, combine the breadcrumbs and Parmesan cheese. Sprinkle the topping over the casserole and bake an additional 5 to 10 minutes, until the topping turns golden brown and the casserole is bubbly.

Sprinkle the casserole with paprika and let stand 10 minutes before serving. It pairs well with rice or pasta.

SAVANNAH OYSTER ROASTS

At the first sign of chill in the air, the people of Savannah and the Lowcountry huddle along riverbanks for the time-honored ritual of roasting freshly harvested oysters. To stage a true Savannah oyster roast, which we do every year at the Delta Plantation, you must invite twenty to thirty of your closest friends, some of whom must love to build fires in open pits. Make sure there are a few sturdy men among them, capable of hoisting large bags of mollusks, and that they don't mind working for their food. It's an honor to hose down and scrub the oysters clean. An even greater one to rake the oysters across the old tin or metal grate atop the fire, cover them with wet burlap sacks, and tend to them, checking every ten minutes for that singular "pop" followed by a "hiss" that announces the oysters are done.

Nearby, picnic and card tables, set end-to-end and blanketed by the day's news, await the first batch. There are stray lemon wedges and containers filled with clarified butter and cocktail sauce scattered about. And the quickest among your pals are already lined up, armed with blunt-edged shucking knives—which are usually nothing but butter knives, tips upturned—and an ice-cold brew.

Drawn from the muddy beds of tidal marshes, these rock-hard bivalves belie the tenderly brined flesh within. It's the slurps of satisfaction that give their secret away.

Sipping Suggestion: Fill a galvanized tub (or several) full of ice, then stock it full of stouts, sparkling wines, Chenin Blancs, and dry-as-a-bone Rieslings. Everyone will be happy.

OYSTERS ROCKEFELLER

Like wine, oysters take on the intricate flavors of their unique climates—in this case, the brine in which they grow in dense clusters. It makes every time you taste an oyster a unique experience. For your next Sunday brunch during the "r" months, try this simple yet sophisticated appetizer.

SERVES 2 TO 4

    24 fresh, unopened live oysters
    2 tablespoons unsalted butter
    1 teaspoon minced garlic
    3 cups fresh spinach leaves
    $1/2$ teaspoon kosher salt
    $1/2$ teaspoon freshly ground black pepper
    6 slices bacon, cooked and crumbled
    $1/4$ cup fine breadcrumbs
    2 cups shredded Italian blend cheese
    Lemon wedges

Place the oven rack in the top position, about 5 inches away from the heating element, and preheat the oven to broil.

Clean and shuck the oysters, and place the half shells with the meats on a broiler pan.

Melt the butter in a sauté pan over medium-high heat. Add the garlic, then the spinach leaves, and cook until the spinach is just wilted. Season the spinach with salt and pepper, and set aside briefly.

Top each half shell with the spinach, a few crumbles of bacon, a teaspoon of breadcrumbs, and a generous sprinkling of cheese.

Broil the oysters for 5 minutes, until the cheese is melted and golden brown. Serve immediately with lemon wedges.

VEGETABLES AND STARCHES

Janet says she married me for my Home Fries (page 147) and my black iron skillets, and I believe her. Until she met me, cooking was a chore for her. In our twenty years together, however, she has discovered the joy of sampling new foods, experimenting with ingredients, and the addicting nature of competition. We love to go on tours with the Southern Foodways Alliance, and make pilgrimages to our purveyor in Atlanta to work on new dishes.

At the shop, Janet takes charge of the sides. Of the two of us, she has developed the more sophisticated palate, and she can tell immediately when something doesn't taste quite right or if one of the cooks has made something without the recipe. She knows when something is missing or is different, and she is a stickler for consistency. She takes as much care with the sides as I do with the meats. A story to illustrate that fact:

One year we were asked to cater a meeting of the National Barbecue Association, which was meeting in Florida. I was cooking for my peers, and I made the best ribs of my life for them. But all of these masters of the pit kept coming up to me and asking about Janet's Favorite Potato Salad (page 156). Not one mention of the ribs! I was a little hurt, to tell you the truth, but when they're shaking your hand and asking you to come back the next year, how hurt can you be?

ALBERTA'S CHICKEN-VEGETABLE SOUP AND CORNBREAD

Like many of the women of her generation, Miss Alberta didn't learn to read or write until much later in life, and she had never written down her recipes. She was an intuitive cook, checking the weather, adjusting ingredients, and tasting as she went. When Miss Alberta was getting on up in years and had retired, we asked her to show us how to make her cornbread and chicken-vegetable soup. Janet got out a notebook (see how important that thing is?) and scribbled down everything thing Miss Alberta did. Miss Alberta then watched (and corrected me) as I repeated her steps.

SERVES 8

> 1 whole 3-pound chicken, giblets removed
> 2 teaspoons sea salt
> 1 teaspoon freshly ground black pepper
> 1 tablespoon olive oil
> $3^1/_2$ to $4^1/_2$ cups water, divided
> 3 (14.5-ounce) cans stewed tomatoes
> 3 large onions, diced
> 3 celery stalks, diced
> 1 carrot, diced
> 1 (16-ounce) bag classic frozen vegetables
> 1 tablespoon uncooked rice

Position a rack in the middle of the oven, and preheat the oven to 350°F.

Rinse the chicken under cool running water, then pat dry.

Sprinkle the salt and pepper evenly over the bird, then rub the seasonings into the skin with the olive oil.

Place the whole chicken in a roasting pan and bake uncovered for $\frac{1}{2}$ hour. Baste the chicken with $\frac{1}{2}$ cup water, then cover and roast for another hour, or until the internal temperature reads 175°F.

While the chicken roasts, start the vegetable soup. In a heavy stockpot over medium heat, combine the stewed tomatoes, 3 cups water, diced onions, celery, carrot, and frozen vegetables. Stir until well combined and bring to a boil. Turn the heat to low and let simmer, covered, until the chicken is done roasting.

Remove the chicken from the oven when it has reached the desired temperature. Add the chicken broth from the roasting pan to the vegetable soup. Add the rice and stir.

When the chicken is cool enough to handle, debone the chicken, making sure to separate all the bones and skin from the meat. Dice the meat and add it to the soup pot. If the soup is too thick, add another cup of water and simmer another $\frac{1}{2}$ hour.

You can serve the soup immediately, but sometimes the flavors meld and taste even better the next day. Store any leftover soup, cooled to room temperature, in an airtight container in the refrigerator for up to 1 week.

CORNBREAD

SERVES 8

> $\frac{1}{4}$ cup vegetable shortening, such as Crisco (Note: Alberta used 2 soupspoons of shortening)
> $1\frac{1}{4}$ cups yellow cornmeal, sifted
> $1\frac{1}{4}$ cups self-rising flour
> $\frac{1}{2}$ to 1 cup whole milk

Position a rack in the lower third of the oven, and preheat the oven to 400°F.

(continued)

Scoop the shortening into an 8-inch cast-iron skillet and melt the shortening in the oven.

While the skillet heats, mix together the cornmeal and flour with a fork, then slowly add the milk until the mixture is the consistency of cake batter.

Once the shortening has melted in the skillet, remove the skillet from the oven using an oven mitt, then pour the cornbread mixture into the skillet.

Return the skillet to the oven and bake for 20 to 25 minutes, or until the cornbread has turned golden brown. Serve immediately.

BARBECUE FOR VEGETARIANS AND VEGANS

For us carnivores, it's hard to imagine a life without meat. The fact remains, however, that 6 to 10 percent of all restaurant patrons in this world are either vegetarians or vegans. Non-meat and non-dairy eaters represent a growing market, and I've found, living and working in a community with an abundance of college students, that the younger the crowd, the higher the population of vegetarians. As caterers and restaurateurs, we must adapt to a variety of appetites.

And meat eaters, don't be fooled by the lack of meat in a dish. That dish can be just as costly to prepare and as hearty as any dish with meat in it. And it can even be tastier.

Many of our recipes are already perfect for vegetarians and vegans—Home Fries (page 147), Green Beans with Garlic (page 168), Smoked Corn on the Cob (without the Cajun Butter) (page 162), and Corn and Black Bean Salad (page 165). Others, such as Savannah Red Rice (page 166), can be easily adapted by removing any meat called for and substituting water or vegetable broth for chicken or beef broth.

HOME FRIES

The dish that won Janet's heart. 'Nough said.

SERVES 6 TO 8

> 5 pounds Idaho potatoes, scrubbed clean and peeled
> $1^1/_2$ cups or more peanut oil
> Seasoning salt

Using a kitchen mandoline or stellar knife skills, julienne the potatoes.

Submerge the potatoes in a bath of ice water.

Fill a deep cast-iron skillet with the peanut oil until it's at least $1/_2$ inch up the sides of the pan. Heat the oil to 350°F.

While the oil is heating, drain a small batch of potatoes on layers of paper towels until they are dry. Repeat with each subsequent batch.

Once the oil has reached the desired temperature, place the first batch of potatoes in the oil, making sure not to overcrowd them. Monitor the potatoes and flip them when the underside is golden brown. Once they are toasted golden all the way through, remove the potatoes with a slotted spoon and drain them on another layer of paper towels on a plate.

Sprinkle the potatoes with seasoning salt, then repeat the process with the next batch of potatoes. If you're like us, each batch of potatoes will disappear long before you can serve them.

BRUNSWICK STEW

In just about every 'cue hall from Miami to Kansas City, you will find Brunswick Stew on the menu. You also will discover as many variations of this hearty soup as there are places that serve it. But I'm here to tell you that there is nothing green in Brunswick Stew. (Read that sentence again, then say it with me just for good measure.) Janet tried for years to perfect this soup, but her results always tasted like beef stew. At one of the cook-offs, my never-shy wife asked a competitor how she made her stew. Although the woman wouldn't share her award-winning recipe, she did share the basic one she had started with and had tweaked over the years to championship status. Well I'm here to tell you, Janet has got it now. Our thick, spicy-sweet, and tomatoey stew is chock full of meat. It's a great way to make use of any leftover brisket, pork, or chicken after a big cookout. Serve it with a side of buttered Cornbread (page 145).

SERVES 8

2 tablespoons butter

1 cup chopped Vidalia onion

2 (14.75-ounce) cans creamed sweet corn

2 cups smoked brisket, pulled or diced

2 cups pulled or diced smoked pork

2 cups pulled or diced smoked chicken

3 cups beef broth

3 cups chicken broth

1 (14.5-ounce) can diced tomatoes

1 (15-ounce) can tomato sauce

4 cups ketchup

2 tablespoons hot sauce

1/4 cup Worcestershire sauce

1/4 cup apple cider vinegar

Juice of 1 freshly squeezed lemon

In a heavy stockpot over medium-high heat, melt the butter and sauté the onions until they become tender.

(continued)

Add the creamed corn, brisket, pork, chicken, and the beef and chicken broths, and stir until well incorporated.

Add the diced tomatoes, tomato sauce, ketchup, hot sauce, Worcestershire sauce, vinegar, and lemon juice, and stir until combined.

Bring the stew to a roiling boil, then turn the heat down to low and let it simmer for 2 hours, stirring occasionally.

You can serve the stew immediately, but sometimes the flavors meld and taste even better the next day. Store any leftover stew, cooled to room temperature, in an airtight container in the refrigerator for up to 1 week.

NO. 1 SPUD

We wanted a stuffed baked potato on our menu, so we started experimenting, but it became a big chore—until a college kid from Memphis shared his technique with us, adapted here. The potatoes are great to throw in the smoker or on the grill when you're smoking a brisket or butt. And you can make Twice-Baked Potatoes (page 152) with any leftovers.

SERVES 4

> 4 large baking potatoes
> Olive oil
> 1 cup various toppings (see below)
> 4 tablespoons unsalted butter, melted, divided
> 4 tablespoons sour cream, divided
> 1 cup melted white cheddar cheese, divided

Scrub and pat the potatoes dry. Rub the potato skins with olive oil, then wrap the potatoes in aluminum foil.

Bring the smoker up to 225°F, then place the wrapped potatoes on the grill plate. After $\frac{1}{2}$ hour, flip the potatoes. Smoke for another $\frac{1}{2}$ hour, then check for tenderness. Keep flipping the potatoes every $\frac{1}{2}$ hour, until they are of the desired consistency and reach 208°F in the center. Remove the potatoes and allow them to cool for 10 minutes.

Wearing gloves, unwrap the potatoes and plate them. Break them open, then top the potatoes with any one of the following:

> Pulled pork with barbecue sauce
>
> Smoked chicken and barbecue sauce
>
> Chopped brisket and chopped green onion

Serve potatoes with melted butter, sour cream, and melted cheese on the side.

TWICE-BAKED POTATOES

An elegant alternative to the meal-in-itself No. 1 Spud (page 151) and the ideal side to the Smoked Prime Rib with Au Jus (page 68).

SERVES 4

> 4 large baking potatoes
> Olive oil
> 4 cups shredded yellow cheddar cheese, divided
> 4 tablespoons unsalted butter, melted
> 4 slices bacon, cooked crisp and crumbled
> 1 bunch green onions, chopped
> 3 teaspoons kosher or sea salt
> 1½ teaspoons freshly ground black pepper
> 1¼ cups sour cream
> 1½ teaspoons paprika

Scrub the potatoes and pat them dry.

Rub the skins of the potatoes with olive oil, then wrap them in aluminum foil.

Bring the smoker up to 225°F, then place the wrapped potatoes on the grill plate. After ½ hour, flip the potatoes. Smoke for another ½ hour, then check for tenderness. Continue smoking the potatoes, flipping them every ½ hour, until they are of the desired consistency.

Remove the potatoes from the smoker and allow them to cool, then cut them in half lengthwise.

Scoop out the inside of each potato and place in a heavy-bottomed pan. Reserve the potato skins and set aside.

Preheat the oven to 350°F. Place the pan of potato insides in the oven and bake until hot, approximately 20 to 30 minutes. Remove the potato insides from the oven and mix with 3 cups cheddar cheese, melted butter, bacon, green onions, salt, and pepper. Add the sour cream and mix until thoroughly combined.

Spoon the potato mixture evenly into the potato skins, then sprinkle each potato with the remaining cheese and the paprika. Cover the potatoes and freeze or refrigerate until ready to serve.

When ready to serve, preheat the oven to 350°F. Place the potatoes on a baking sheet and bake, uncovered, until the cheese has melted and the tops of the potatoes have browned. Serve hot.

GROWN-UP MAC 'N' CHEESE

I'm not one for elbow macaroni forever mortared by layers of bright orange cheddar. I like a creamier, more sophisticated version of this meat-and-three standard—one that can stand up to meat eaters without their feeling deprived, and also satisfy vegetarians and children.

SERVES 12

1 pound dry rigatoni
3 cups whole milk
1 cup heavy cream
3 sprigs fresh thyme
2 cloves garlic, peeled and smashed
3 tablespoons unsalted butter
3 tablespoons all-purpose flour
5 cups shredded sharp white cheddar cheese, divided
1 teaspoon freshly ground black pepper
1 cup shredded fresh Parmesan cheese
1/4 cup chopped flat-leaf parsley

Position a rack in the middle of the oven, and preheat the oven to 400°F. Butter a 9-by-13-inch baking dish and set aside.

Cook the rigatoni according to package instructions.

In another small saucepan over medium heat, warm the milk, cream, thyme, and garlic until just before boiling. Carefully remove any solid remnants of the thyme and garlic from the milk mixture.

In a large, deep skillet, melt the butter over medium heat. Whisk in the flour for 1 minute, stirring constantly, then add the milk mixture while continuing to stir until the sauce is smooth and thickened.

Stir in 4 cups of the white cheddar cheese and continue to stir until the cheese is completely melted. Season with pepper.

Add the cooked and drained rigatoni, and stir to coat all of the noodles.

Pour the cheesy noodles into the prepared baking dish. Sprinkle the top with the remaining cheeses, then bake the mac 'n' cheese for 30 minutes, until it is hot and bubbly.

Remove the pan from the oven and sprinkle with the parsley. Serve immediately.

> Tip: You can make the mac 'n' cheese a day or two ahead. Just store it, uncooked and covered, in the refrigerator and bake just before serving.

JANET'S FAVORITE POTATO SALAD

When Janet moved from up North to Atlanta, she discovered a whole new world of flavors. She loves a Southern-style potato salad with the richness of hard-boiled eggs and the sweet-tart interplay of pickles. To craft her signature ladies-who-lunch dish, she combined two other recipes she had been experimenting with: one from the back of a Hellmann's mayonnaise jar and the other from The Kansas City Barbeque Society Cookbook. *She's pretty happy with the results.*

SERVES 12

> 6 medium potatoes, peeled and cubed
> 1¹/₂ cups mayonnaise, preferably Hellmann's
> 2 tablespoons champagne vinegar
> 2 tablespoons Dijon mustard
> 1 tablespoon yellow mustard
> 1¹/₂ teaspoons fine sea salt
> 1 teaspoon sugar
> 1 teaspoon freshly ground black pepper
> 5 hard-boiled eggs, finely chopped
> 4 whole sweet pickles, such as gherkins, finely chopped
> 1 medium onion, finely chopped
> 1 cup thinly sliced celery
> Paprika

In a 4-quart saucepan, cover potatoes with cold water and bring to a boil over medium-high heat. Reduce the heat to medium and cook until the potatoes are tender. Drain and cool the potatoes to room temperature.

In a small bowl, mix together the mayonnaise, vinegar, mustards, salt, sugar, and black pepper until well combined.

Once the potatoes have sufficiently cooled, gently mix together the potatoes, eggs, pickles, onion, and celery in a large bowl. Pour the mayonnaise mixture over the potatoes and stir until well coated.

Cover the bowl with plastic wrap and chill the potato salad for at least 2 hours so that the flavors will meld together.

Serve chilled with a sprinkling of paprika.

Store leftovers in an airtight container in the refrigerator for up to 3 days.

> **Tip:** Ever the time-saving multitasker, Janet boils her eggs and potatoes at the same time by putting the eggs on top of the potatoes in the boiling water.

SWEET POTATO CASSEROLE

Well, I'm going to have to eat my words right about now. There are a couple of recipes that Janet and I have been forbidden to share with anyone. One recipe is the potato salad we serve in the restaurant; the other is our Dutch Sweet Potato Casserole. Both recipes came from my Uncle Oscar, who lives in Memphis, Tennessee. I'm going to honor his request that these recipes remain in the family, because he's family. But I promise I'll pass them along before I die. In the meantime, our cowriter Amy shared her Aunt Barbara's recipe—the one her aunt has brought to every Thanksgiving celebration since 1978. Amy included it in the cookbook she wrote for her family as a Christmas present. She thinks it comes pretty close to Uncle Oscar's top-secret dish.

SERVES 8

FOR THE TOPPING:

> 1 cup firmly packed light brown sugar
>
> 1 cup chopped pecans
>
> $^1/_2$ cup all-purpose flour
>
> $^1/_3$ cup melted butter

FOR THE FILLING:

> 3 cups sweet potatoes (approximately 4 large
>   sweet potatoes), cooked and peeled
>
> $^1/_2$ cup granulated sugar
>
> 8 tablespoons unsalted butter
>
> 2 eggs, beaten
>
> $^1/_3$ cup whole milk
>
> 1 teaspoon pure vanilla extract

Position a rack in the middle of the oven, and preheat the oven to 350°F. Prepare a 9-by-13-inch baking dish with butter or a nonstick cooking spray.

In a medium bowl and using a fork, mix together the brown sugar, pecans, flour, and melted butter until well combined. Set aside.

In a large bowl, mash together the sweet potatoes, sugar, butter, eggs, milk, and vanilla until well combined.

Spread the potato mixture evenly into the prepared baking dish, then sprinkle the topping over the potato mixture, covering the entire surface.

Place the baking pan in the oven and bake for 25 minutes, or until the topping has turned golden brown. Serve immediately.

WILEY'S FAVORITE BBQ BEANS

Every now and then I get bored with a dish, and that's how I came up with my version of baked beans. These beans have a little less sweet and a bit more kick. Smoking them intensifies their flavor, and depending on the wood, imparts subtle variations in taste. So I encourage you to experiment. Sometimes I turn up the volume by tossing in some pulled pork or pieces of brisket.

SERVES 12

1 (28-ounce) can baked beans

1 (15.5-ounce) can black beans, rinsed and drained

1 (15.5-ounce) can kidney beans, rinsed and drained

1 cup The **Q** Company's Basic **BBQ** Sauce (page 42)

1 cup firmly packed light brown sugar

1 cup diced onions

1 cup diced green bell peppers

¹/₃ cup canned tomatoes, preferably Ro-tel Original Diced Tomatoes & Green Chilies

¹/₃ cup Dijon mustard

Bring your smoker up between 325°F and 375°F.

In a 3-quart saucepan, combine all the ingredients. Stir until well combined.

When you are ready to cook the beans, set the pan on the grill away from the direct heat. Cover the grill and smoke for no less than 30 minutes, or until the beans are hot, bubbly, and you get the desired amount of smoke flavor you're after. Serve immediately.

Once cooled, store the beans in an airtight container in the refrigerator for up to 3 days.

SMOKED CORN ON THE COB WITH CAJUN BUTTER

Fresh corn on the cob, especially Silver Queen corn, tastes like summer—sweet and juicy. Smoking corn with woods such as pecan, cherry, or applewood intensifies its flavor. A few ears don't take up too much room on the grill's surface, so toss a few in over indirect heat a couple of hours before the brisket or pork butt are done. The fresher the corn, the better the results. Make sure you smoke the corn within a day or two of buying it, unless you're lucky enough to pick it right from the field. The embellished butter spices things up a bit.

SERVES 8

> 8 fresh ears of corn, still in the husk
> 1 pound (4 sticks) unsalted butter, melted
> 3 tablespoons finely chopped fresh cilantro
> $1^1/2$ teaspoons chili powder
> $1^1/2$ teaspoons lime zest
> $^3/_4$ teaspoon sea salt
> $^3/_4$ teaspoon ground cumin
> $^1/_4$ teaspoon garlic powder

Soak the ears in cold water for at least 2 hours, preferably overnight.

Prepare the smoker or grill for indirect cooking on low heat, between 220°F and 250°F.

Remove the ears from the water, rinse then pat dry.

Place the ears in the smoker or over indirect heat, leaving space between the ears for the heat to circulate. Smoke for $1^1/2$ to 2 hours.

Just before serving the corn, combine the butter, cilantro, chili powder, lime zest, salt, cumin, and garlic powder in a medium bowl and mix well. Serve it alongside the corn with a brush to slather the ears when they are done.

(continued)

To store any leftover corn, either wrap the ears in foil and store in the refrigerator or remove the husks, trim the kernels from the cob, and use for Smoked Cream Corn (below).

SMOKED CREAM CORN
Classic comfort food.

> **4 ears Smoked Corn on the Cob (page 162)**
> **4 tablespoons unsalted butter**
> **$^{1}/_{2}$ teaspoon sea salt**
> **$^{1}/_{8}$ teaspoon freshly ground black pepper**
> **1 tablespoon all-purpose flour**
> **$^{3}/_{4}$ cup half-and-half, plus more if necessary**

Trim the kernels from the ears of corn and reserve.

In a large skillet, melt the butter over medium heat, then add the kernels, salt, and pepper. Cook for 5 minutes, stirring constantly to make sure the corn doesn't brown.

Sprinkle the corn with flour and cook 2 minutes more. Add the half-and-half, stirring and simmering until the corn is tender. Add more half-and-half if the corn is too thick. Serve immediately.

CORN AND BLACK BEAN SALAD

When Janet invites her friends over for a summer lunch, she almost always serves this salad. Cool, crisp, and flavor-filled. If you have any smoked corn from the Smoked Corn on the Cob with Cajun Butter recipe (page 162) left over, use it for the corn called for in this recipe. It also makes a fine salsa for a grilled mahimahi. Kick up the color and taste by adding 1 cup of diced smoked salmon.

SERVES 8

2 cups corn, fresh, canned, or frozen

2 cups cooked black beans, rinsed and drained

2 cups red wine vinegar

1 cup coarsely chopped fresh fruit, such as
    mango, peach, or cantaloupe

1 large red bell pepper, finely chopped

$^1/_2$ large red onion, finely chopped

Juice of 1 lime

Salt and pepper

In a large bowl, combine all the ingredients. Taste and add salt and pepper as needed.

Cover the bowl with plastic wrap and chill in the refrigerator for at least 2 hours to allow the flavors to meld. Store in an airtight container in the refrigerator for up to 3 days.

SAVANNAH RED RICE

This dish has been a staple of Savannah tables since the days when rice was the Lowcountry's cash crop. There are different versions of it, some with shrimp and more akin to gumbo. In our shop, we owe this version of the dish to Marion, our pit master and an all-around great cook. Even in the baking sun, working a smoking pit, Marion never loses his cool.

SERVES 4 TO 6

> ¹⁄₄ pound (about 6 slices) applewood-smoked
>   bacon, cut into pieces
> ¹⁄₂ cup chopped onions
> 1¹⁄₂ pounds smoked sausage, cut into ¹⁄₂-inch slices
> 2 cups diced tomatoes
> 2 cups tomato sauce
> 2 cups long grain rice

Preheat the oven to 350°F.

Spray a 9-by-13-inch baking dish with nonstick cooking spray and set aside.

Brown the bacon pieces in a large heavy-bottomed pan until crisp. Remove the bacon from the skillet and drain on paper towels.

In the remnant bacon grease, sauté the onions until they are tender and translucent, about 5 to 7 minutes. Toss in the sausage and lightly brown, then stir in the diced tomatoes and tomato sauce. Bring to a light boil.

Stir in the rice about ¹⁄₂ cup at a time, until all the rice is incorporated and soaking up the sauce.

Pour the rice into the prepared baking dish and bake for 30 to 40 minutes, until the rice is tender and the top has slightly browned. Remove the dish from the oven and let stand for 10 minutes. Serve immediately.

BLACK BEANS AND YELLOW RICE

This Caribbean-influenced specialty, which comes by way of our pit master Marion, makes a great side to Smoked Bone-in Pork Loin (page 98), Smoked Cornish Game Hens (page 109), and Citrus Shrimp (page 126).

SERVES 4 TO 6

    1 ($^{1}/_2$-pound) bag dried black beans
    2 tablespoons olive oil
    1 teaspoon sea salt
    $^{1}/_2$ teaspoon freshly ground black pepper
    1 tablespoon ground cumin
    $^{1}/_2$ medium green bell pepper, diced
    $^{1}/_2$ medium red bell pepper, diced
    1 medium onion, diced
    3 cups yellow rice
    6 teaspoons (1 ounce) Better Than Bouillon Chicken Base

Rinse the black beans in a colander under cold running water.

Place the beans in a large stockpot over high heat, and cover with water by at least 2 inches. Add olive oil, salt, pepper, cumin, bell peppers, and onion. Bring the beans to a boil, then turn down the heat to low and simmer until the beans are tender.

While the beans simmer, place the rice in a medium heavy-bottomed saucepan and cover with water by $^{1}/_2$ inch. Add the chicken base and stir. Bring the rice to a boil over high heat, then reduce the heat to low, cover the rice, and cook until the rice is tender and all the water is absorbed. Keep the rice warm until the beans are ready.

To serve, spoon $^{1}/_2$ cup of rice onto a plate and spoon the beans over the top.

GREEN BEANS WITH GARLIC

I like salty, slow-simmered green beans flavored with bacon as much as the next guy, but I love the bright freshness and subtle flavors this side provides. It is the perfect accompaniment to Smokehouse Meatloaf (page 70) when served alongside boiled new potatoes sprinkled with feta cheese.

SERVES 8

> 2 pounds whole green beans, fresh or frozen
> 2 tablespoons vegetable oil
> 2 tablespoons sea salt
> 1 tablespoon minced garlic in oil

Fill a 4-quart pan with water and bring it to a boil over high heat. Place the green beans in the water, and bring it back to a boil. Blanch the green beans for 5 minutes.

Strain the beans, which should appear bright green.

Place the beans in a large bowl and toss with the oil, salt, and garlic. Serve immediately.

Store leftovers in an airtight container in the refrigerator for up to 3 days.

COLESLAW

The debate between a creamy coleslaw and a tangy vinegar one causes almost as many arguments as beef or pork, mustard or ketchup, or pecan versus mesquite. Again, I like them all—I'm an equal opportunity slaw-er. I like to pile a spoonful of this peppery blend on a pulled pork sandwich, just like they do in St. Louis. As an aside, the dressing makes a great brining liquid.

SERVES 8

> 1¹/₂ tablespoons canola oil
> 1¹/₂ teaspoons celery seed
> ¹/₂ teaspoon sea salt
> ¹/₂ teaspoon freshly ground black pepper
> ¹/₂ teaspoon finely minced garlic
> 2 cups apple cider vinegar
> 2 cups granulated sugar
> 1 (16-ounce) package coleslaw mix

In a medium bowl, combine the oil, celery seed, sea salt, black pepper, and garlic, then mix until oil and seasonings are well combined. Slowly stir in the vinegar until well combined. Then add the sugar and stir until the sugar is completely dissolved.

Cover the bowl with plastic wrap and chill the dressing for at least 2 hours so that the flavors will meld together.

Just before serving, pour the slaw mix into a large bowl, then toss with the dressing. By waiting until the last minute to toss, you'll ensure that your slaw is crisp and cool.

COLLARD GREENS

Janet's initiation into Southern cuisine was a bit fraught. When she and I lived in Atlanta, we entertained frequently. Not long after we married and were celebrating our first New Year's Day together, I bought her a big bushel of fresh collard greens so that she could make a batch to go with the traditional black-eyed peas, while I smoked the ribs. Nothing says love like a fresh bouquet of collards, right?

She didn't much like the cleaning and cutting, and that first batch turned out stinking awful . . . literally. The next year she gave it another try, but made me cook them outside. They were as dismal as the first batch. The next year Janet asked one of her teacher colleagues how she made hers. We managed to choke those down.

By the fourth year, Janet discovered—much to her consternation and my punishment— that collard greens came packaged already cut and washed. This discovery, however, buoyed her spirits for another attempt. She added some sugar, hot sauce, and ham hocks, and her greens finally were edible. She kept fiddling with the recipe for about ten years until she found the right chemistry. For Janet, conquering collards was a victory.

SERVES 8

> 8 cups water
>
> $3^1/2$ pounds fresh collard greens, cleaned, stemmed, and roughly chopped
>
> 1 pound smoked ham hocks
>
> 3 large onions, chopped
>
> 1 medium red bell pepper, seeded and chopped
>
> 1 medium green bell pepper, seeded and chopped
>
> $3/4$ cup granulated sugar
>
> $2/3$ cup apple cider vinegar
>
> 1 tablespoon honey
>
> 3 cloves garlic, finely minced
>
> 1 tablespoon freshly ground black pepper
>
> $1/2$ teaspoon hot sauce

2 teaspoons celery seed
2 teaspoons sea salt
1^1/$_2$ teaspoons baking soda

In a large, heavy-bottomed stockpot, combine all ingredients. Simmer, covered, for 2 hours, stirring occasionally.

With a slotted spoon, remove the ham hocks. When the ham hocks are cool enough to handle, pick the meat from them and put the bits back into the greens.

Simmer another 15 minutes. You can serve the greens immediately, but sometimes the flavors meld and taste even better the next day.

Store any leftover greens, cooled to room temperature, in an airtight container in the refrigerator for up to 1 week.

SQUASH CASSEROLE

This casserole is one of Janet's and my favorite dishes. When we first opened the restaurant, we served it as one of our sides. We noticed, though, that by the end of the lunch rush the vibrant yellow of the summer squash had mellowed, as had the flavors. It's just one of those dishes that needs to be served right out of the oven. We took it off the menu, yet we still get requests for it. We serve it at home often.

SERVES 8

> 4 pounds yellow squash, sliced
>
> 1 medium Vidalia onion, chopped
>
> 2 cups crushed cornflakes
>
> 1 (10.5-ounce) can cream of mushroom soup
>
> 4 tablespoons unsalted butter, melted
>
> 1 teaspoon freshly ground black pepper
>
> 1 teaspoon sea salt
>
> 1 cup shredded white cheddar or Monterey Jack cheese

Position a rack in the middle of the oven, and preheat the oven to 350°F. Butter a square 9-by-9-inch baking pan, then set aside.

In a 3-quart saucepan, combine the squash and onion. Cover with salted water and cook over medium heat until the squash turns fork tender, approximately 20 minutes.

Remove the squash from the heat and drain off the water. Mash the squash and onions in the saucepan. Add the cornflakes, soup, butter, pepper, and salt, then mix until all ingredients are well incorporated.

Transfer the squash mixture to the baking pan and sprinkle the casserole with the cheese.

Bake approximately 20 minutes, until the cheese is melted and the mixture is hot and bubbly. Serve immediately.

GRILLED ASPARAGUS

If you want something quick and impressive as a side, you can't do any better than Grilled Asparagus. I make these at home all the time, and we serve them in the restaurant with our Smoked Prime Rib with Au Jus (page 68) on Saturday nights. For special occasions, I'll wrap a portion size in bacon before I put them on the grill. The versatile marinade is good for almost any vegetable that you can grill.

SERVES 4

> 1 cup soy sauce
> 1 cup olive oil
> $^1/_2$ cup sesame oil
> 1 pound asparagus
> Salt and pepper

Combine the soy sauce, olive oil, and sesame oil in a gallon-sized zip-lock plastic bag. Set aside.

Rinse the asparagus under cool water, then drain on paper towels.

Trim the dry bottoms from the asparagus and discard, or freeze the bottoms for the future when you want to make a vegetable stock.

Toss the asparagus with salt and pepper, then place the asparagus in the marinade bag, close, and marinate in the refrigerator overnight.

Prepare the grill for direct heat.

Remove the asparagus from the marinade and place in a vegetable basket for grilling. Reserve the marinade for a dipping sauce. Grill on one side for 12 minutes, flip, and then grill for 12 minutes more. Serve immediately.

SMOKED STUFFED PORTOBELLO MUSHROOMS

They'll probably make me hand in my carnivore card when I admit that a portobello mushroom is sometimes as satisfying as a steak—especially when smoked with applewood. Janet and I first tried this recipe at home and liked it so much we added it to our catering menu. It's a huge hit with the vegetarian customers, and it's a great dish to sneak in a lot of healthy vegetables with a lot of flavor for those meat-only eaters.

SERVES 4

FOR THE MARINADE:

- $1/2$ cup soy sauce
- $1/2$ cup olive oil
- $1/2$ cup water
- 1 tablespoon Worcestershire sauce
- 1 tablespoon minced garlic
- 4 portobello mushrooms, cleaned and stems removed

FOR THE STUFFING:

- 1 green bell pepper, diced into $1/4$-inch pieces
- 1 red bell pepper, diced into $1/4$-inch pieces
- 1 yellow bell pepper, diced into $1/4$-inch pieces
- $1/2$ large purple onion, diced into $1/4$-inch pieces
- 1 large beefsteak tomato, diced into $1/4$-inch pieces
- $1/2$ teaspoon sea salt
- $1/2$ teaspoon freshly ground black pepper
- 1 cup shredded provolone, mozzarella, or Swiss cheese

Combine the soy sauce, olive oil, water, Worcestershire sauce, and garlic in a heavy-duty plastic bag with a secure closure. Place the portobello mushroom caps in the bag and seal it tight.

(continued)

Put the bag in the refrigerator and let the mushrooms marinate for at least 8 hours, or overnight.

Bring the smoker up to between 220°F and 250°F.

While the grill heats, remove the mushrooms from the plastic bag and lay them top side down on a plate.

Mix together the peppers, onion, tomato, salt, and pepper in a medium bowl.

Spoon equal amounts of the vegetable mixture into the mushroom caps.

Place the mushroom caps on the grill, carefully avoiding any direct heat, and cover. Let the mushrooms smoke for 45 minutes, until they soften and turn dark.

Remove the mushrooms from the grill and sprinkle each with ¼ cup of cheese. The cheese will melt from the warmth of the mushrooms. Serve immediately.

> **Tip:** Because the portobello mushroom is meaty, it works well in a sandwich. Try serving these stuffed mushrooms on onion buns slathered with mayonnaise or Cajun Rémoulade (page 135), lettuce, and fresh sliced or Fried Green Tomatoes (page 177).

FRIED GREEN TOMATOES

I don't know if it's because of the movie or book with the same name, but our Fried Green Tomatoes are a huge hit with tourists who come from outside of the South. And I've discovered that you can gussy up any sandwich or dish that calls for a slice of tomato with these sweet, crunchy bites.

SERVES 4

> 4 large green tomatoes, sliced ³/₄-inch thick
> 2 large eggs, beaten
> 2 tablespoons water
> 1 package Zatarain's Seasoned Fish Fry Breading Mix
> Oil, preferably peanut or canola, for frying

Drain the tomato slices on paper towels.

Mix the eggs and water in a shallow dish, and place the breading mix in another dish.

In a large cast-iron skillet, Dutch oven, or deep fryer, add enough oil to cover the tomato slices and heat to 350°F.

Dip each tomato slice in the egg wash, then lightly dust each slice with the breading.

Fry the tomato slices until they are golden brown all around.

Drain the slices on paper towels, then serve hot with a side of Cajun Rémoulade (page 135).

FRIED PICKLES

There's an urban legend floating around Savannah that pregnant women who are nearing or past their due dates can speed up their child's arrival by partaking of our Fried Pickles. We'll know if it's true the day someone goes into labor in our restaurant. Maybe they'll name their newborn after me.

SERVES 4

>2 cups crinkle-cut dill pickle slices, drained
>1 cup jalapeño juice
>1¹/₂ cups all-purpose flour
>Fine sea salt
>Freshly ground black pepper
>Cayenne pepper
>Garlic powder
>Oil, preferably peanut or canola, for frying

Brine the pickle chips in the jalapeño juice in an airtight container overnight.

Drain the pickles on a couple of layers of paper towels.

Season flour to taste with salt, black pepper, cayenne pepper, and garlic powder. Place the seasoned flour in a gallon-sized zip-lock plastic bag.

In a large cast-iron skillet, Dutch oven, or deep fryer, add enough oil to cover the pickles, and heat to 350°F.

Toss the pickles in the flour, then fry them until they are golden brown all around.

Drain the pickles on paper towels, then serve them hot with a side of Cajun Rémoulade (page 135) or ranch dressing spiked with jalapeño juice.

SATURDAY ONION RINGS

The venerable Vidalia onion grows just a couple of counties away from Savannah, which means we are blessed with the fresh harvest from April to June every year. The Vidalia's nature lends itself perfectly to fried onion rings, as do Texas and Walla Walla sweet onions. I like to dip these in cool, creamy ranch dressing or our spicy Cajun Rémoulade (page 135).

SERVES 4

> 5 to 6 large Vidalia onions
> 1½ cups all-purpose flour
> Fine sea salt
> Freshly ground black pepper
> Garlic powder
> 1 teaspoon baking powder
> 1 egg, beaten
> 16 ounces beer, preferably a Pabst Blue Ribbon tall boy
> Milk, to thin the batter if necessary
> Oil, preferably peanut or canola, for frying

Peel and slice the onions into at least ½-inch rings. Separate the rings and lay them on a paper towel to dry.

Season flour to taste with salt, pepper, and garlic powder. In a bowl, mix together the seasoned flour and baking powder until well combined. Add the egg and beer, then mix the batter thoroughly. Add milk by the teaspoon to thin, if necessary.

In a large cast-iron skillet, Dutch oven, or deep fryer, add enough oil to cover the rings and heat to 350°F. Dredge the onion rings in the batter, then fry them until they are golden brown all around.

Drain the onion rings on paper towels, then serve them hot.

BLACK-EYED PEA HUMMUS

This recipe is a decidedly Southern twist on the Mediterranean version. It's a surprising and savory dip for crudités and pita chips—something new for your next party. This dish, along with Pimento Cheese (page 75), has become a staple of our coauthor Amy's Christmas Eve celebration.

MAKES 3¹/₃ CUPS

> 4 sprigs fresh cilantro
> 4 sprigs fresh parsley
> ³/₄ cup diced onion
> 3 cups cooked and cooled black-eyed peas, drained
> ¹/₂ cup roasted red peppers
> ¹/₄ cup tahini
> 2 tablespoons white balsamic vinegar
> 2 tablespoons Dijon mustard
> 1 tablespoon freshly squeezed lemon juice
> 1 teaspoon celery salt
> 1 teaspoon light soy sauce
> ¹/₂ teaspoon ground cumin
> Sea salt and freshly ground black pepper, to taste

Coarsely chop the cilantro, parsley, and onion in a food processor. Add the remaining ingredients and blend until smooth.

Serve with crudités and toasted slices of baguette. It's also a great accompaniment to the Deep South Antipasti Platter (page 77).

> Tip: Make the hummus a day or two ahead of the party and store in an airtight container in the refrigerator so that the flavors can meld together. Bring the hummus to room temperature before serving.

SUGAR, BUTTER, AND FLOUR

Is it just a Southern thing, or does everyone crave a little something sweet at the end of every meal, even breakfast? Growing up, my mom would make the pound cake recipe from Irma Rombauer's *Joy of Cooking* and serve it with fresh strawberries and blueberries. Nothing fancy—just good, honest eats.

Maybe that is why I return to the simple, reassuring pleasures of my childhood when it comes to desserts—with little tweaks thrown in here and there, like a praline-sauced bread pudding made with thick slabs of buttered Texas toast, or shortbread cookies in a banana pudding, or peanut butter pie uplifted by whipped cream *in* the filling. I eat strawberry shortcake only when the berries are sugared by a late frost and plumped by the spring sun.

Sweet finishes are just that; they make you linger over conversation, share, and end on a high note.

GRILLED PEACHES

You know it's summer in Savannah when the roadside stands stake hand-painted signs heralding the arrival of peaches. Next to eating one fresh off the tree with the juice running down your chin, grilled peaches strike the perfect finish to the sweet heat of barbecue. Served alongside homemade ice cream, they're a succulent warm-weather treat.

SERVES 4

> 2 tablespoons butter
> 1 cup orange blossom, sourwood, or wildflower honey
> 1 tablespoon vanilla extract
> $1/2$ teaspoon ground cinnamon
> 4 fresh peaches, halved and pitted, skins on
> Vegetable oil

In a medium saucepan over medium heat, melt the butter and stir in the honey, vanilla, and ground cinnamon until the sauce is smooth and glossy. Turn the heat to low and keep warm.

Meanwhile, set up the grill for direct heat, and bring it up to between 350°F and 400°F.

Brush the peach halves all over with vegetable oil and grill the peaches, flesh side down, for 4 minutes. Turn the peaches skin side down and grill for 1 more minute.

Serve the peaches immediately with a scoop of homemade ice cream and drizzled with the honey sauce. Enjoy, and don't be afraid to lick the plate to get every last juicy bit.

PEACH ICE CREAM

This recipe recalls those cookouts on hot summer days at Lake Lanier when my family would churn sweet cream with a hand-cranked machine tucked in by rock salt. That's one tradition that needs to come back, because every luscious bite is worth the work and the wait!

MAKES 1 GALLON

2$^{1}/_{2}$ cups light whipping cream
2 cups whole milk
$^{3}/_{4}$ cups granulated sugar
$^{1}/_{8}$ teaspoon salt
1 teaspoon pure vanilla extract
$^{1}/_{4}$ teaspoon almond extract
2 large eggs, beaten
6 to 8 fresh peaches, peeled, pitted, and mashed
$^{3}/_{4}$ cup granulated sugar

In the canister of an ice cream maker—I prefer the old-fashioned kind—combine the cream and the milk. Stir in the sugar, salt, vanilla and almond extracts, and eggs.

In a separate bowl, combine the mashed peaches and sugar.

Add the peach mixture to the cream mixture.

Follow the directions for your particular ice cream maker until you have a thick, rich, and cool treat.

Eat alone in a bowl, or scoop to accompany Grilled Peaches (page 184) and Pound Cake (page 187).

POUND CAKE

A friend gave a copy of her mother's pound cake recipe to Janet for her birthday one year. Now it's our go-to recipe for a sublime finish to any meal. I like to serve it with fresh fruit.

MAKES 1 LOAF

$^1/_2$ pound (2 sticks) unsalted butter, room temperature
3 cups granulated sugar
6 large eggs
$2^2/_3$ cups all-purpose flour
$^1/_2$ teaspoon baking soda
$^1/_2$ teaspoon salt
1 cup sour cream
1 teaspoon vanilla extract

Preheat the oven to 325°F. Prepare a standard loaf pan with butter and flour, making sure to tap out any excess flour. Set the pan aside.

Using a stand mixer with a paddle attachment, cream the butter on medium speed. Add the sugar $^1/_4$ cup at a time and beat until light and fluffy. Then add the eggs one at a time until they are well incorporated. Scrape down the sides of the bowl, if necessary.

In a separate bowl, sift together the flour, baking soda, and salt. Sift again.

With the mixer on low speed, add the flour mixture to the butter mixture in thirds, alternating with the sour cream, until the flour mixture and sour cream are well incorporated. Add the vanilla, then beat for 2 minutes more.

Pour the batter into the prepared loaf pan and bake for 1 hour and 20 minutes, until golden brown and it springs back to the touch.

Let the pan cool for 10 minutes before removing the pound cake and letting it cool on a wire rack. Slice and serve.

CHOCOLATE-BOURBON-PECAN PIE

The kick of Kentucky bourbon in this pie makes me giddy. The smoky, caramel undertones bring out the woodsy warmth of Georgia pecans and strengthen the chocolate. It sure goes down good after a plate of brisket and a glass of red wine, followed by a Don Mateo Natural cigar.

SERVES 8

> 1 prepared piecrust, such as Pillsbury Pie Crusts

FOR THE FILLING:

> 4 large eggs
> 1 cup light corn syrup
> 6 tablespoons butter, melted
> $1/2$ cup granulated sugar
> $1/4$ cup firmly packed light brown sugar
> 3 tablespoons Kentucky bourbon
> 1 tablespoon all-purpose flour
> 1 tablespoon pure vanilla extract
> 1 cup coarsely chopped pecans
> 1 cup semisweet chocolate chips, plus additional for garnish

Position a rack in the lower third of the oven, and preheat the oven to 350°F. Fit the piecrust to a 9-inch pie plate. Fold and crimp any excess dough around the edges.

In a large bowl, whisk together the eggs, corn syrup, butter, sugars, bourbon, flour, and vanilla until well combined. Stir the pecans and chocolate chips into the filling mixture, then pour the filling into the piecrust.

(continued)

Place the pie in the oven and bake for 1 hour, or until set. The pie filling may jiggle a bit in the middle, but if you smell a strong chocolate scent, you'll know the pie is done. Remove from the oven and set aside to cool.

Serve each slice of pie with a scoop of your favorite vanilla or butter pecan ice cream, and a sprinkle of chocolate chips.

Store the pie in an airtight container at room temperature for up to 3 days.

STRAWBERRY SHORTCAKE

In the Southeast, strawberries are best from February through May. Janet inherited this recipe from her mother, and we use it in the restaurant during those glorious months when strawberries are ripe, red, juicy, and naturally sweet.

SERVES 4

4 cups fresh strawberries, hulls removed, sliced
$1/2$ cup granulated sugar
$2^1/3$ cups Bisquick
$1/2$ cup milk
3 tablespoons granulated sugar
3 tablespoons unsalted butter, melted
2 cups heavy whipping cream
2 teaspoons pure vanilla extract

Mix the strawberries and sugar in a large bowl, then set aside to macerate.

Preheat the oven to 425°F, and line a baking sheet with parchment paper.

In a medium bowl, stir together the Bisquick, milk, sugar, and butter until a soft dough forms. Using a medium ice cream scoop, drop the biscuits onto the baking sheet about 2 inches apart.

Bake the biscuits for 10 to 12 minutes, until golden brown. Remove the biscuits from the oven and place them on a wire rack to cool.

When the biscuits have cooled, mix the whipping cream and vanilla on high speed until soft peaks form.

To assemble the shortcakes, cut each biscuit in half, then place the bottom of the biscuit on a plate. Spoon 1 cup strawberries over each biscuit, then place the other half of the biscuit on top. Crown it with a generous portion of the whipped cream. Drizzle with a teaspoon of the strawberry juice.

PEANUT BUTTER PIE

Our version of this down-home dessert resulted from a series of happy accidents. The original recipe came from our next-door neighbor in Savannah. It called for bananas and we named it "The Elvis." Based on customer feedback, we dropped the bananas and created a shortbread crust, using the leftover cookies from the Banana Pudding recipe (page 194). That crust proved a little too salty up against the peanut butter and too tough to cut, so we substituted a chocolate cookie crust—to overwhelmingly positive results. On a particularly busy day, our dessert cook whipped the cream and folded it into the pie filling instead of piping it on top. She inadvertently created a pie with a mousse-like texture that's not cloyingly sweet. We—better yet, our guests—love it!

SERVES 8

FOR THE CRUST:

> 40 Oreo cookies
> 8 tablespoons (1 stick) unsalted butter, melted

FOR THE FILLING:

> 1 cup firmly packed light brown sugar
> 1 (8-ounce) package cream cheese, softened
> $3/4$ cup creamy peanut butter, preferably Jif
> $1^1/2$ to 2 cups heavy whipping cream

FOR THE TOPPING:

> 2 cups heavy whipping cream
> 2 teaspoons vanilla extract
> Chocolate syrup
> $1/4$ cup coarsely chopped honey-roasted peanuts (optional)

Place the cookies in a food processor and pulse until they are ground into a coarse meal.

Pour the cookie crumbs into a medium bowl and combine the crumbs with the melted butter. Press the cookie mixture into the bottom of a 10-inch springform pan and set aside.

To make the filling, use a stand mixer with a paddle attachment on medium speed. Beat together the brown sugar, cream cheese, and peanut butter until light and fluffy. Set aside.

In another bowl, using an electric hand mixer with a whisk attachment, whip the cream on high speed until light and fluffy.

Fold the whipped cream into the peanut butter mixture until even and airy. Spread the filling onto the cookie pie crust and chill in the refrigerator for at least 2 hours.

For the topping, mix the heavy whipping cream and vanilla on high speed until soft peaks form. Spread the whipped topping like a meringue over the top of the chilled pie filling.

To serve, slice the pie into eight equal pieces, then plate, drizzle with chocolate syrup, and sprinkle with chopped peanuts if you like.

Store the pie in an airtight container in the refrigerator for up to 3 days.

> Tip: This pie freezes well, so you can make it a couple of days ahead, thaw it, then top it with the whipped cream.

BANANA PUDDING

Nothing tastes like Southern comfort more than a creamy bowl of banana pudding. It's perfect for a potluck or Sunday supper. In our kitchen, I draw the line at vanilla wafers and instant pudding. We bake our own shortbread cookies. And the custard recipe is courtesy of our good friend Damon Lee Fowler, a fine food historian and cookbook author in his own right. His original recipe calls for meringue, but our kitchen is so hot, it would never hold up. We top it with whipped cream instead.

SERVES 8

FOR THE SHORTBREAD COOKIES:

$3^1/2$ cups all-purpose flour

$1/4$ teaspoon sea salt

$3/4$ pound (3 sticks) unsalted butter, room temperature

1 cup granulated sugar, plus additional for sprinkling

1 teaspoon pure vanilla extract

FOR THE VANILLA CUSTARD:

5 large egg yolks

$1^1/3$ cups granulated sugar

$1/2$ cup all-purpose flour

3 cups whole milk

1 teaspoon pure vanilla extract

FOR THE WHIPPED CREAM:

2 cups heavy whipping cream

$1/4$ cup granulated sugar

4 ripe bananas, sliced into $1/4$-inch-thick coins

Position a rack in the middle of the oven, and preheat the oven to 350°F.

Line a baking sheet with parchment paper.

Sift together the flour and salt in a medium bowl, then set aside.

Beat the butter, sugar, and vanilla in the bowl of a stand mixer fitted with a paddle attachment until they are just combined. Slowly add the flour mixture and mix on low speed until the cookie dough comes together.

Turn the dough onto a floured work surface and shape it into a flat round. Wrap it in plastic wrap and chill in the refrigerator for 30 minutes.

Using a rolling pin, roll the dough to a $\frac{1}{2}$-inch thickness. Using a 1-inch round biscuit cutter, shape the cookies and place them on the baking sheet at least 2 inches apart. Repeat until all the dough has been used.

Place the pan in the oven and bake for 20 to 25 minutes, until the edges begin to brown. Remove the cookies from the oven and allow them to cool.

Meanwhile, make the vanilla custard. Beat the egg yolks until smooth and set them aside.

Create a double boiler by placing a heatproof bowl over a heavy-bottomed medium-sized saucepan with $\frac{1}{2}$ inch of simmering water in the bottom.

In the bowl, mix the sugar and flour together. Slowly add the milk and bring the mixture to a boil, stirring constantly. Remove the double boiler from the heat.

Temper the eggs by vigorously mixing $\frac{1}{2}$ cup of the hot milk mixture into the yolks, then slowly add the eggs into the remaining mixture in the bowl.

Return the double boiler to the heat and cook until thickened, stirring constantly, about 5 to 8 minutes.

Remove the mixture from the heat and stir in the vanilla until well incorporated. Set the custard aside to cool.

(continued)

While the custard cools, whip the cream and sugar on high speed with an electric mixer until airy and firm.

To assemble the pudding in a trifle bowl or other clear glass dish, create the first layer with the shortbread cookies, breaking the cookies into pieces to fill any gaps. Follow with a layer of banana slices, then custard, then whipped cream. Repeat, multiple times if needed to use the ingredients, always ending with the whipped cream on top. If you have any cookies left over, you can crumble them over the top. Serve immediately.

BREAD PUDDING WITH PRALINE-BOURBON SAUCE

Necessity once again is the mother of invention. Bread pudding wasn't initially on our menu, but we realized we were pitching a lot of unused Texas toast at the end of every day. Janet suggested we use it in her bread pudding recipe—sans raisins and studded with meaty Georgia pecans. The result is a sweet, buttery concoction, almost as addictive as barbecue.

SERVES 6

4 eggs
$3/4$ cup ($1^1/_2$ sticks) unsalted butter, melted
$1^3/_4$ cups sugar
$1^1/_2$ teaspoons vanilla
$1^1/_2$ teaspoons ground cinnamon
$1^1/_2$ teaspoons ground nutmeg
1 cup whole milk
1 cup heavy cream
$1/3$ cup chopped pecans
6 cups roughly cubed Texas toast
$1/4$ cup firmly packed light brown sugar
Praline-Bourbon Sauce (page 199)

Preheat the oven to 350°F.

Butter a 9-by-13-inch baking pan or dish. Set aside.

In the bowl of a stand mixer, beat the eggs on medium speed for 30 to 45 seconds, until the eggs are lemon yellow in color. Add the butter, sugar, vanilla, cinnamon, and nutmeg, then mix on medium speed until thoroughly combined. Scrape down the sides of the bowl, then add the milk and cream. Mix on medium speed until thoroughly combined. Fold in the pecans.

(continued)

Fill a large bowl with the bread cubes and pour the egg-cream mixture over the bread. Fold the ingredients until the bread absorbs the liquid.

Transfer the soaked bread to the prepared baking pan, then sprinkle the top with the brown sugar.

Place the pan in the oven and bake for 25 to 35 minutes, until the bread pudding is firm and golden brown.

Remove the pan from the oven and let stand for 10 minutes to cool.

Cut the pudding into squares and serve with a healthy drizzle of Praline-Bourbon Sauce.

PRALINE-BOURBON SAUCE
Deep caramel notes.

> 8 tablespoons (1 stick) unsalted butter, room temperature
> 1 cup granulated sugar
> 1/4 cup water
> 1 egg yolk
> 2 tablespoons good-quality Kentucky bourbon

Combine the butter, sugar, water, and egg yolk in a heavy-bottomed saucepan over medium heat. Mix well and cook until all the sugar is dissolved. Reduce the heat to low and continue cooking until the mixture starts to thicken, about 3 minutes.

Remove the mixture from the heat and stir in the bourbon.

Serve warm over the Bread Pudding (page 197).

LIBATIONS

There's an old saying around here that the first question they ask you in Atlanta is, What do you do? In Augusta, Where do you worship? In Charleston, Who are your people? And in Savannah, What do you drink?

Although sweet tea may be the house wine of the South, Savannah is known for her cocktails. She likes a party. So did my mother, who served a particularly rich and potent eggnog every Christmas—without nutmeg, thank you very much. And Janet has perfected her own version of Chatham Artillery Punch: a wicked Firewater Punch (page 203).

Me? Well, you can tell that I like to cook with bourbon. But I like to sip an icy glass of Wiley's Sangria (page 204). It makes the sweltering summer afternoons here pass with greater ease.

WILEY'S LEMONADE

We serve this sweet, tart thirst-quencher in the restaurant and on our catering menu. Some folks like to mix it half-and-half with ice tea for an Arnold Palmer.

MAKES 3 GALLONS

$1^1/2$ gallons cold water
11 cups granulated sugar
$9^1/2$ cups ReaLemon juice
Juice of 3 freshly squeezed lemons
2 lemons, sliced into $1/4$-inch-thick rounds

Combine the water, sugar, and juices in a five-gallon container and stir until all the sugar has dissolved.

To serve, pour the lemonade into a pitcher over ice and garnish with the lemon slices.

> Tip: For a refreshing lemonade just for grown-ups, fill a tall glass with crushed ice, add 1 ounce of champagne, vodka, peach schnapps, or any other liquor of choice, then top with the lemonade. Enjoy responsibly.

FIREWATER PUNCH

This recipe comes from Janet, who made this potent punch for her son Ben's christening. She lived in a two-hundred-year-old colonial house in Massachusetts at the time. It was undergoing some renovations on the porch, and there was a thirty-inch drop between the landing and the millstone used as the first step. Well, the family priest took several nips of the punch and fell flat out the front door trying to make his way down. It packs a wallop!

MAKES 1 GALLON

> 1 cup freshly squeezed lemon juice (approximately 12 lemons)
> 2 cups maraschino cherry juice
> 1 cup curaçao
> 2 cups brandy
> 1 to 2 bottles Champagne, Prosecco, Cava, or other sparkling wine
> 2 (16-ounce) bottles soda water
> Powdered sugar, to taste
> Maraschino cherries, for garnish

In a large punch bowl, combine the lemon juice, cherry juice, curaçao, and brandy.

Just before serving, stir in one bottle of Champagne and soda water. Mix well and sample to test for balance and sweetness. Add 1 tablespoon powdered sugar and 1 cup Champagne at a time until you get the desired balance.

Serve each drink with a cherry for garnish.

> **Tip:** You can freeze the maraschino cherries along with frozen whole strawberries in an ice mold, then float the ice mold in the punch bowl. It'll do double duty as a pretty centerpiece that keeps the punch cold.

WILEY'S SANGRIA

As far as alcohol is concerned, we only serve beer and wine in the shop, and on occasion I want a little something different. Those occasions usually occur at the height of July and August, when sangria makes the perfect summer sipper—cool and crisp. Make sure to serve it in a big goblet with a slice of orange and plenty of ice.

MAKES ¹/₂ GALLON

> 1 bottle (750 milliliters) red wine, preferably
>   Cabernet Sauvignon or Merlot
> Juice of 2 lemons
> Juice of 2 oranges
> Juice of 2 limes
> 8 tablespoons sugar
> 2 shots brandy
> 4 cups Sprite
> 1 lemon, cut into ¹/₄-inch slices, seeds removed
> 1 orange, cut into ¹/₄-inch slices, seeds removed
> 1 lime, cut into ¹/₄-inch slices

In a large pitcher, combine the red wine, fruit juices, sugar, and brandy. Stir well and set in the refrigerator for at least 3 hours, but preferably overnight, so that the flavors can meld together.

Add Sprite and fruit slices just before serving in chilled glasses filled with ice.

> **Tip:** Just like barbecue, you can improvise here according to seasons and tastes. Use white wine, peaches, blueberries, and strawberries in early summer. For fewer calories, use soda water instead of Sprite.

MIMI'S EGGNOG

Every year at our Christmas Eve celebrations, my mother, Mimi, would make a big production out of making her eggnog. She would count every damn egg as she cracked it; likewise, every tablespoon of "buh-uh-bun," as she pronounced it in her proper Buckhead drawl. She always served it in a freshly polished sterling punch bowl with sterling cups.

MAKES 12 CUPS

>12 fresh eggs, separated
>12 tablespoons sugar
>12 tablespoons bourbon
>1 pint heavy cream

In a large bowl, beat the egg whites until stiff but not dry.

In another large bowl, beat the egg yolks with the sugar until the sugar has dissolved and the mixture is pale and frothy. Add the bourbon and mix well.

Stir the egg whites into the yolk mixture until well combined, then stir in the cream until well combined.

Chill in the refrigerator for at least 2 hours, then serve.

HELPFUL RESOURCES

Have you succumbed to the 'cue addiction yet? If you've read this far, it won't be long before you do—and I'm happy to enable you as much as possible by telling you where to find others who share your passion, as well as where to find the implements and products to help you master grilling and smoking.

And if you ever find your way to Savannah, come on into our little shop on Whitemarsh Island. I'll be the guy at the end of the bar, chewing on a cigar and sitting in a director's chair that reads "The BBQ General." I'd be delighted to talk barbecue with you.

BARBECUE AND FOOD ORGANIZATIONS

Kansas City Barbeque Society

(800) 963-5227

www.kcbs.us

Founded in 1985, the KCBS recognizes barbecue as America's cuisine, and strives to preserve it as an art form and play it like a sport. The KCBS counts more than 15,000 members worldwide, making it the largest organization devoted to barbecue networking, trend tracking, promotion, and archival research. It is responsible for officially sanctioning barbecue competitions and certifying judges, who must repeat the following oath:

> "I do solemnly swear to objectively and subjectively evaluate each Barbeque meat that is presented to my eyes, my nose, my hands and my palate. I accept my duty to be an Official KCBS Certified Judge, so that truth, justice, excellence in Barbeque and the American Way of Life may be strengthened and preserved forever."

Memphis Barbecue Network

www.mbnbbq.com

The Memphis Barbecue Network prizes flavor above all in its officially sanctioned cook-offs and competitions. Its "Memphis in May" is one of the largest and most prestigious barbecue cooking contests in the nation. It coincides with the Beale Street Music Festival, combining two distinctively delicious American art forms—blues and 'cue.

National Barbecue Association

(888) 909-2121

www.nbbqa.org

The National Barbecue Association provides support and networking opportunities for barbecue professionals, including marketing and design services. It promotes the "art and enjoyment" of barbecue.

Southern Foodways Alliance

(662) 915-3368

www.southernfoodways.com

The nonprofit, membership-based Southern Foodways Alliance studies with academic rigor the food cultures of the American South through oral history, research, independent study, documentaries and films, and symposia. Its goal is to give voice to the voiceless in food culture (shrimpers, farmers, cooks, etc.).

WILEY'S READING LIST

Chile Pepper Magazine

www.chilepepper.com

Kansas City Barbeque Society Bullsheet

Note: You must be a member of the KCBS to receive the *Bullsheet*. To join, go to www.kcbs.us/join.php to fill out an application, or contact the KCBS by sending an e-mail to bullsheet@kcbs.us.

National Barbecue News

www.barbecuenews.com

WILEY'S FAVORITE COOKBOOKS

BBQ USA, Barbecue! Bible, and *Planet Barbecue!* by Steven Raichlen

Championship Barbecue and *Championship Barbecue Sauces* by Paul Kirk

Dr. BBQ's Big-Time Barbecue Cookbook by Ray Lampe

Fish & Shellfish, Grilled & Smoked by Karen Adler and Judith M. Fertig

The Kansas City Barbecue Society Cookbook: 25th Anniversary Edition by Ardie Davis, Paul Kirk, and Carolyn Wells

Peace, Love, and Barbecue by Mike Mills and Amy Mills Tunnicliffe

WHERE WE BUY OUR SUPPLIES

GRILLS AND SMOKERS

Big Green Egg
(770) 938-9394
www.biggreenegg.com

Southern Pride
(731) 696-3175
www.southern-pride.com

Weber
(800) 446-1071
www.weber.com

TOOLS OF THE TRADE

Kitchenware Outfitters
(912) 356-1117
www.kitchenwareoutfitters.com

CLAMS, MUSSELS, AND OYSTERS

Bluffton Oyster Company
(843) 757-4010
www.blufftonoyster.com

Taylor Shellfish Farms
(360) 426-6178
www.taylorshellfishfarms.com

SHRIMP AND OTHER SEAFOOD

Dubberly's Seafood
(912) 925-6433
www.sweetsavannahshrimp.com

Nelson's Quality Shrimp Company
(912) 897-1123
www.facebook.com/pages/
NELSONS-QUALITY-SHRIMP-
COMPANY/111618848850177

Charles J. Russo's Seafood
(912) 234-5196
www.russoseafood.com

BACON AND COUNTRY HAM

Benton's Smoky Mountain Country Hams
(423) 442-5003
www.bentonscountryhams2.com

SPICES AND SEASONINGS

Dekalb Farmers Market
(404) 377-6400
www.dekalbfarmersmarket.com

HONEY

Savannah Bee Company
(800) 955-5080
www.savannahbee.com

WHERE TO BUY WILEY'S SAUCES AND RUBS

Mo Hotta Mo Betta
(800) 462-3220
www.mohotta.com

ACKNOWLEDGMENTS

We know that we're only able to do what we do because of the generosity and talents of so many others—first and foremost, our loyal customers and treasured guests who visit us every time they're in Savannah. We offer our deepest gratitude to Marion Woodberry, Terry Mooney, and the rest of our crew at Wiley's Championship BBQ for helping us fulfill the dream of opening an award-winning restaurant that fills peoples' bellies and keeps them coming back. Without your hard work, dedication to consistency and customer service, and enduring friendship, we would not be able to keep the doors open.

Thanks to Janet Cochran, aka "Buckhead Janet," who sweated out many a competition by our sides as a valued member of The Q Company. We'd be remiss if we didn't also thank Sandra and David Stuart, as well as many others, who all pushed us to get better with every contest.

This book would not have been possible without the faith and enthusiasm of Madge Baird and Bob Cooper, our editors at Gibbs Smith. Many thanks for whipping this book into shape, encouraging our ideas, and assembling a top-notch creative team. Andrew Brozyna, you've designed a lovely package here. We are in awe of the dynamic duo of photographer Chia Chong and stylist Libbie Summers, who confirm that we eat with our eyes first—and we want to eat these pages.

Many thanks to Judge Stanley F. Birch and Adam Kirk for their guidance on legal matters entirely new to us. And thanks to our son, Ben Morgan, for his eagle-eyed copyediting, and his lovely wife, Leslie Slavich, for testing recipes and asking the hard questions.

Thanks to Claude Auerbach at Savannah's gourmet cheese shop, FORM, for the wine and craft beer pairing suggestions. We can't wait to try every last one of them, and hope you'll join us in doing so. We also greatly appreciate the help of Christine Fournier, who tested recipes under the guise of family dinners and let us know that they met and exceeded her daddy's expectations.

Amy, in particular, would like to thank the Savannah Scribes—Katherine

Oxnard Ellis, Judy Fogarty, Lyn Gregory, Tina Kelly, and Nancy Remler—for their early readings and thoughtful critiques of the manuscript. Ditto to Dr. James Lough, Dr. Beth Concepcíon, and Professor Lee Griffith, her graduate committee in the writing program at the Savannah College of Art and Design, for indulging a cookbook proposal as a final thesis. Many thanks to Cheryl and Griffith Day for taking a gamble on a first-time author, and to her colleagues at *Savannah* magazine for their encouragement and support. Love and big hugs to her mom for helping with the cooking and cleaning while she worked on this book, and to her husband, Brian, for being such a willing guinea pig in the kitchen.

I would be remiss if I didn't thank the good people at Weber—the makers of the equipment on which I learned to grill and smoke—who started this revolution we call barbecue. More than fifty years after the invention of the kettle, Weber products are still kicking butt in competitions.

I've used Southern Pride wood-burning smokers every day for the past twenty years, and I have to say they take the labor out of work. I appreciate not having to get up at three in the morning to stoke the fires.

And finally, thanks to Mike Mills for giving us the idea for our shop's name. He is among one of my favorite cookbook authors and fellow 'cue addicts. My shelves runneth over with books that have inspired and challenged me. I hope this book does the same for you and shares a place of pride upon your shelf.

ABOUT THE AUTHORS

Wiley McCrary grew up in the food business. His grandfather founded Atlanta's Massey & Fair food brokerage in 1929, where Wiley started his career as a retail merchandiser in 1967. When the company was acquired by Archer Daniels Midland sixteen years later, Wiley branched out and founded his own business dedicated to his true love: barbecue. Wiley's Atlanta Barbecue and Catering Company quickly established itself as the go-to caterer for businesses and parties around Atlanta. After his wife, Janet, grew tired of his talking about competing on the barbecue competition circuit "someday," he entered a contest at Stone Mountain, Georgia, under The Q Company moniker. He won second place in ribs and became addicted to hearing his name called out in competition. He and Janet found mentors in Ed and Muriel Roith of Happy Holla BBQ out of Kansas City, and they spent a couple of years traveling around the competition circuit with the Roiths to learn the ins and outs of presentation, judging, and the subculture that is

barbecue. Wiley and Janet competed for thirteen years, winning many awards. In 2005, they "retired" to Savannah, Georgia, and opened a small restaurant on Whitemarsh Island called Wiley's Championship BBQ, where they serve competition barbecue to thousands of customers.

For the first forty years of her life, **Janet McCrary** lived in a culinary wasteland. Although she was never undernourished, she was never accused of gastronomic aptitude. Cooking was a job—something that had to be done to survive. That all changed the day she met Wiley, who taught her that cooking was an act of love and cause for celebration. Through competitions, catering, and classes, Janet developed a sophisticated palate. She now delights in surprising friends and family—most of whom remember when she thought grilling meant hot dogs—with the various dishes she makes. In her spare time, Janet enjoys walking with her rescue dogs, Izzy and Misty, knitting sweaters during football season for her grandchildren, and making Nantucket lightship baskets.

Amy Paige Condon has crabbed muddy riverbanks with a Gullah diva, sampled hundreds of froyo combinations in the dead of winter, and rubbed the bellies of pastured pigs—all in pursuit of the stories behind the foods served on our tables. As the associate editor of the award-winning *Savannah* magazine, she has written about food, home and design, and fashion, and has profiled chefs, authors, and other personalities. Amy coauthored *The Back in the Day Bakery Cookbook* with bakery owners Cheryl and Griffith Day, which was named one of Amazon.com's top ten cookbooks of 2012, recognized by *Food & Wine* as one of the best cookbooks of 2013, and named Cookbook of the Year by the Southern Independent Booksellers Alliance. Her work has appeared in *The Local Palate* and the *National Barbecue News*. A native Texan and Miami transplant, Amy resides in Savannah, Georgia, with her husband, Brian, and their two mutts, Harper and Barkley. When she's not writing, she's cooking up something.

INDEX OF RECIPES

Alberta's Chicken-Vegetable Soup and
Cornbread, 144
Appetizers
Black-Eyed Pea Hummus, 181
Crab-Stuffed Mushrooms, 136
Deep South Antipasti Platter, 77
Fried Pickles, 178
Janet's Crab Cakes with Cajun Rémoulade,
133
Oysters Rockefeller, 141
Pimento Cheese, 75
Redneck Nachos, 90
Saturday Hot Wings, 108
Apricot Marinade, 31
Asparagus, Grilled, 173
Au Jus, 69

Banana Pudding, 194
Basic BBQ Sauce, The Q Company's, 42
Basic Poultry Marinade, 29
Basic Rub, The Q Company's, 34
Beans, Wiley's Favorite BBQ, 161
Beef
Brunswick Stew, 148
Burnt Ends, 54
Deep South Antipasti Platter, 77
French Dip Sandwich, 69
Honky Tonk Sandwich, 59
Patty Melt, 72
Perfect Steak with Wiley's Special
Mushrooms, 60
Q Company's Brisket, The, 52

Smoked Beef Tenderloin with Roquefort
Sauce, 63
Smoked Corned Beef Reuben, 56
Smoked Prime Rib with Au Jus, 68
Smokehouse Meatball and Pimento Cheese
Sandwich, 73
Smokehouse Meatloaf, 70
Spaghetti on the Grill, 76
Tri-Tip, 66
Wrap Two Ways: Black and Blue Wrap, 54
Wrap Two Ways: Brisket Wrap, 54
Beer BBQ Sauce, Big Jim's, 46
Beverages
Firewater Punch, 203
Mimi's Eggnog, 205
Wiley's Sangria, 204
Black Beans and Yellow Rice, 167
Black-Eyed Pea Hummus, 181
BLT, Ultimate, 94
Bone-In Pork Loin, Smoked, 98
Bread Pudding with Praline-Bourbon Sauce, 197
Brisket, The Q Company's, 52
Brunswick Stew, 148
Burnt Ends, 54

Cajun Rémoulade, 135
Cajun Rub, 38
Club, Smokehouse, 92
Cod with Garlic Butter, Black Iron Skillet, 124
Coleslaw, 169
Collard Greens, 170
Cuban Sandwich, 99

Chicken
    Alberta's Chicken-Vegetable Soup and
        Cornbread, 144
    Basic Poultry Marinade, 29
    Brunswick Stew, 148
    Q Company's Chicken, The, 102
    Q Company's Chicken Marinade, The ,30
    Saturday Hot Wings, 108
    Smoked and Stuffed Chicken Breasts, 107
    Smoked Chicken Two Ways: Smoked Chicken
        Salad, 105
    Smoked Chicken Two Ways: Smoked Fried
        Chicken, 105
Chocolate-Bourbon-Pecan Pie, 188
Citrus Shrimp, 126
Corn and Black Bean Salad, 165
Corn on the Cob with Cajun Butter, Smoked, 162
Cornbread, 145
Corned Beef Reuben, Smoked, 56
Cornish Game Hens, Smoked, 109
Crab Cakes with Cajun Rémoulade, Janet's, 133
Crab-Stuffed Mushrooms, 136
Cream Corn, Smoked, 164
Cuban Sandwich, 99

Deep-Fried Turkey, 114
Deep South Antipasti Platter, 77
Desserts
    Banana Pudding, 194
    Bread Pudding with Praline-Bourbon Sauce,
        197
    Chocolate-Bourbon-Pecan Pie, 188
    Grilled Peaches, 184
    Peach Ice Cream, 186
    Peanut Butter Pie, 192
    Pound Cake, 187
    Praline-Bourbon Sauce, 199
    Strawberry Shortcake, 191

Eggnog, Mimi's, 205

Firewater Punch, 203
Fish
    BBQ Salmon with Shallot-Dill Sauce, 119
    Black Iron Skillet Cod with Garlic Butter, 124
    Smoked Salmon and Corn Salad, 122
French Dip Sandwich, 69

Garlic-Pepper Rub, 37
Green Beans with Garlic, 168
Green Tomatoes, Fried, 177

Home Fries, 147
Honky Tonk Sandwich, 59
Hot Wings, Saturday, 108

Lamb
    Grilled Rack of Lamb with Orange
        Marmalade Glaze, 80
    Lamb Marinade, 33
    Lamb Rub, 39
    Smoked Leg of Lamb, 83
Lemonade, Wiley's, 202
Lemon-Pepper Rub, 36
Lobster with Crab in Cream, Grilled, 137

Mac 'n' Cheese, Grown-Up, 154
Marinades
    Apricot Marinade, 31
    Basic Poultry Marinade, 29
    Lamb Marinade, 33
    Q Company's Chicken Marinade, The, 30
    Q Company's Pork Injection, The, 40
    Wiley's Rib Spray, 41
Meatball and Pimento Cheese Sandwich,
    Smokehouse, 73
Meatloaf, Smokehouse, 70
Mojo Sauce, 32
Mushrooms, Wiley's Special, 62

Nachos, Redneck, 90
North Carolina Sauce, Wiley's, 47

Onion Rings, Saturday, 180
Orange Marmalade Glaze, 82
Oysters Rockefeller, 141

Patty Melt, 72
Peach Ice Cream, 186
Peaches, Grilled, 184
Peanut Butter Pie, 192
Pickles, Fried, 178
Pimento Cheese, 75
Pork
    Brunswick Stew, 148
    Cuban Sandwich, 99
    Deep South Antipasti Platter, 77
    Patty Melt, 72
    Q Company's Pork Injection, The, 40
    Q Company's Pulled Pork, The, 86
    Q Company's Ribs, The, 95
    Redneck Nachos, 90
    Smoked Bone-In Pork Loin, 98
    Smokehouse Club, 92
    Smokehouse Meatball and Pimento Cheese
        Sandwich, 73
    Smokehouse Meatloaf, 70
    Spaghetti on the Grill, 76
    Ultimate BLT, 94
    Wiley's Rib Spray, 41
Portobello Mushrooms, Smoked Stuffed, 174
Potato Salad, Janet's Favorite, 156
Potatoes, Twice-Baked, 152
Poultry Marinade, Basic, 29
Pound Cake, 187
Praline-Bourbon Sauce, 199
Prime Rib with Au Jus, Smoked, 68
Pulled Pork, The Q Company's, 86

Q Company's Chicken, The, 102

Q Company's Chicken Marinade, The, 30
Q Company's Pork Injection, The, 40

Rack of Lamb with Orange Marmalade Glaze,
    Grilled, 80
Red Rice, Savannah, 166
Ribs, The Q Company's, 95
Roquefort Sauce, 65

Rubs
    Cajun Rub, 38
    Garlic-Pepper Rub, 37
    Lemon–Pepper Rub, 36
    Q Company's Basic Rub, The, 34

Salads
    Coleslaw, 169
    Corn and Black Bean Salad, 165
    Shrimp Salad, 132
    Smoked Chicken Two Ways: Smoked Chicken
        Salad, 105
    Smoked Salmon and Corn Salad, 122
Salmon and Corn Salad, Smoked, 122
Salmon with Shallot-Dill Sauce, BBQ , 119
Sandwiches
    Cuban Sandwich, 99
    French Dip Sandwich, 69
    Honky Tonk Sandwich, 59
    Patty Melt, 72
    Smoked Corned Beef Reuben, 56
    Smokehouse Club, 92
    Smokehouse Meatball and Pimento Cheese
        Sandwich, 73
    Ultimate BLT, 94
    Wrap Two Ways: Black and Blue Wrap, 54
    Wrap Two Ways: Brisket Wrap, 54
Sangria, Wiley's, 204
Sauces and Condiments
    Au Jus, 69
    Big Jim's Beer BBQ Sauce, 46

Cajun Rémoulade, 135
Mojo Sauce, 32
Orange Marmalade Glaze, 82
Pimento Cheese, 75
Praline-Bourbon Sauce, 199
Q Company's Basic BBQ Sauce, The, 42
Roquefort Sauce, 65
Shallot-Dill Sauce, 121
Texas Outback BBQ Sauce, 49
Wiley's North Carolina Sauce, 47
Wiley's South Carolina Sauce, 48
Seafood Casserole, 138
Shallot-Dill Sauce, 121
Shellfish
Citrus Shrimp, 126
Crab-Stuffed Mushrooms, 136
Grilled Lobster with Crab in Cream, 137
Janet's Crab Cakes with Cajun Rémoulade, 133
Janet's Shrimp 'n' Grits, 130
Oysters Rockefeller, 141
Seafood Casserole, 138
Shrimp Salad, 132
Shrimp 'n' Grits, Janet's, 130
Shrimp Salad, 132
Side Dishes
Black Beans and Yellow Rice, 167
Coleslaw, 169
Collard Greens, 170
Corn and Black Bean Salad, 165
Cornbread, 145
Fried Green Tomatoes, 177
Fried Pickles, 178
Green Beans with Garlic, 168
Grilled Asparagus, 173
Grown-Up Mac 'n' Cheese, 154
Home Fries, 147
Janet's Favorite Potato Salad, 156
No. 1 Spud, 151
Saturday Onion Rings, 180

Savannah Red Rice, 166
Smoked Corn on the Cob with Cajun Butter, 162
Smoked Cream Corn, 164
Smoked Stuffed Portobello Mushrooms, 174
Squash Casserole, 172
Sweet Potato Casserole, 158
Twice-Baked Potatoes, 152
Wiley's Favorite BBQ Beans, 161
Wiley's Special Mushrooms, 62
Smoked Beef Tenderloin with Roquefort Sauce, 63
Smoked Chicken Two Ways: Smoked Chicken Salad, 105
Smoked Chicken Two Ways: Smoked Fried Chicken, 105
Smoked Leg of Lamb, 83
Smoked Turkey, 110
Soups and Stews
Alberta's Chicken-Vegetable Soup and Cornbread, 144
Brunswick Stew, 148
South Carolina Sauce, Wiley's, 48
Spaghetti on the Grill, 76
Spud, No. 1, 151
Squash Casserole, 172
Steak with Wiley's Special Mushrooms, Perfect, 60
Strawberry Shortcake, 191
Stuffed Chicken Breasts, Smoked and, 107
Sweet Potato Casserole, 158

Texas Outback BBQ Sauce, 49
Tri-Tip, 66
Turkey
Smoked Turkey, 110
Deep-Fried Turkey, 114

Wrap Two Ways: Brisket Wrap, 54
Wrap Two Ways: Black and Blue Wrap, 54